BERLITZ

IRELAND

- A  in the text denotes a highly recommended sight
- A complete A–Z of practical information starts on p.115
- Extensive mapping on cover; Blueprint map on p.115

Although we make every effort to ensure the accuracy of the information in this guide, changes do occur. If you have any new information, suggestions or corrections to contribute, we would like to hear from you. Please write to Berlitz Publishing at one of the above addresses.

Original text:	Ken Bernstein
Additional text:	Hugh Oram, Sinéad Doody
Editors:	Nicola Gadsby, Sarah Hudson
Photography:	Pete Bennett
Layout:	Cristina Fino Silva
Cartography:	*Falk* Falk-Verlag, Hamburg

Cover photograph: Dalkey Island, © Berlitz
p. 4 photograph: Achill Bay, © Berlitz

CONTENTS

Ireland and the Irish

The grass grows greener in Ireland – it's not called the 'Emerald Isle' for nothing, although the verdant pastures alternate with plains of grain, bleak, rugged hills, mountains and soggy bogs.

The quick-changing sky of this unspoiled Atlantic island only adds to the drama of the encounter between land and sea. You will never be further than 70 miles (113km) from Ireland's spectacular 3,000-mile (4,800km) coastline rising from white sand coves to form some of Europe's most dramatic cliffs. Meanwhile, inland, at least one of the country's 800 lakes and rivers is usually within sight.

Ireland's tiny size doesn't lead to delusions of grandeur, but there's plenty of room to breathe, and air worth breathing on this, the world's 20th largest island.

Scattered amidst the many natural beauties of the country stand impressive stone relics which date back thousands of years, while in the foreground, enhancing all the other attractions, are the handsome, hospitable people of Ireland. They call foreign travellers 'visitors' rather than 'tourists', and offer a typically warm and generous 'hundred thousand welcomes'.

Two-thirds of the island's nearly five million inhabitants live in the 26 counties of the Republic of Ireland. The six counties of Northern Ireland remained a part of the United Kingdom when the island was partitioned after World War I in an attempt to solve the ongoing 'Irish problem'.

The majority of the people in the Republic of Ireland are Catholic, but in the North the majority is Protestant, with its strongest loyalties to Britain. Years of 'troubles' in Ulster have scarred several northern towns, but the countryside still remains unscathed. Life in the Republic continues to be as relaxed as ever; the policemen strolling down the streets are unarmed, and the most serious danger to life and limb comes **5** from zigzagging, or at worst from the country's erratic and unconventional drivers.

Aside from unworried motorists and the mounting problem of traffic in larger towns, driving in rural Ireland can still represent an old-fashioned pleasure. The open road helps contribute to the overall feeling of well-being – not quite apathy or tropical torpor, but the ability to put life's little problems into perspective.

Those eager colonialists, the Romans, never could conquer Ireland, nor did they attempt to, thus isolating Hibernia (as they named it) from the rest of Western European civilization. However, invaders and immigrants from other lands arrived to temper the early Celtic culture. When King Brian Boru turned on the Vikings in 1014, his brief victory for the Irish was only the beginning of nine centuries of suffering and the struggle for independence.

The historic Anglo-Norman conquest of Ireland in the year 1169 paved the way for the supremacy of English over the **6** colourful Gaelic of the natives.

Nowadays barely one in a hundred people in Ireland speaks Irish more fluently than English. However, the revival of Gaelic, which is actually an Indo-European language, has become state policy; it is now taught in schools and printed (along with English) on all official signs and documents.

Although everyday use of Gaelic is in practice limited to the Gaeltacht area – the small pockets of culture predominantly in the west of the island, its vocabulary and intonation have moulded the distinctive, lilting form of English spoken in Ireland. Eloquence in English is not merely confined to great Irish authors and playwrights; almost everybody in Ireland seems to be a witty, articulate coversationalist.

Though a species of palm tree thrives in many an Irish garden, you'd hardly mistake Ireland for a tropical paradise. Nonetheless, the proximity of the Gulf Stream keeps winter mild. Snow is rare, rain is not. Significant rainfall is recorded for about three out of every four days near the west coast,

and for every second day in the east. The level of downpour varies enormously, and ranges from stormy torrents to refreshing mist which is so nebulous it leaves the pavement unmarked. The sun is never far behind the rain, however, and the slightest shower has always been a fine excuse for an Irish rainbow.

The best way to see Ireland is by car, with the most inviting beach maybe just at the end of a spur-of-the-moment tour. Coach tours cover all the main highlights with the usual stops for browsing, shopping,

*W*atch the sheep farmers at market or enjoy charming Dublin from a horse-drawn landau.

eating and drinking, and the drivers usually functioning as guides who, being Irish, tend to be convivial.

If sightseeing by rental car or coach is too fast for your taste, you can change the pace and point of view by settling aboard a horse-drawn gypsy caravan, or perhaps spending a week aboard a rented cabin cruiser on a gently idling river odyssey. If you have never captained a boat, they'll teach you. Even those tired of the conventional hotel room can

seek out castles renovated as hotels, farmsteads, guesthouses or quaint thatched cottages.

Sightseers who prefer cities won't be disappointed either, because in Dublin, a capital of broad avenues, green parks, and harmonious and ordered terraces, there is more in the way of museums, galleries and other cultural attractions than many cities its size. The River Liffey cuts through the heart of the city to the sea, and indeed all Ireland's major towns derive their character from the sea or rivers or both. Belfast, the metropolis of the north, is Ireland's biggest port, while Cork, the Republic's second city, was founded in ages past by the Vikings on an island of the River Lee. In the west, the River Shannon explains and beautifies the city of Limerick.

By and large, however, the truly inspiring sights of Ireland are found outside the big towns. Indeed, the concept of a town is not much more than a thousand years old. Before then Ireland was almost entirely rural and the most evocative parts of it's ancient buildings

were tranquil, not to say isolated settlements of a monastic nature. In fact, the setting is more often than not an intrinsic part of the unique quality of the monument.

Natural wonders in Ireland can be as awesome as the Cliffs of Moher, or as tranquil as the lakes of Killarney, as

*R*emnants of Ireland's past, the whitewashed cottage (left) is often finished off with a colourful window box (above).

mystical as the 'holy mountain' of Croagh Patrick, or as delightful as the horse-breeding prairie of the Curragh. On the way from one place to another, you can savour more modest, but no less memorable pleasures of Ireland: the sight of sheep nibbling the heather, or sails seizing the wind on a cool *lough* (lake), or freckled farm children waving.

The great outdoors is where everything happens here. Between the rivers, the lakes and the sea, there's something exciting for every kind of fisherman. Sailing and boating share top billing. While the sea does not get any warmer than what might optimistically be called 'refreshing', there'll be splashing about and sunbathing at hundreds of beaches.

Horses figure prominently, with many stables to choose from if you're thinking of a riding holiday. Those who admire horses from afar – and Irish horses are admired the world over – can go to the races. The green Irish terrain is also ideal for golf, and there **10** are around 300 courses.

If possible, try to catch the national game, 'hurling', said to be the fastest field-game in the world.

Shopping is rewarding in Ireland, where handicrafts sell themselves; if the salesmanship were more relaxed, the shops might just as well shut down. Friendly service also features in the pleasant activities of eating and drinking in Ireland. The chefs use some of the world's best meat and fish, so they tend not to worry about fancy recipes, and the local whiskey and stout are well-deserving of their far-flung fame.

With a glass of something local in your hand, listen to delightful, traditional Irish ballads in an old wood-panelled pub. Concerts go on all year round, and in the land of the great playwrights Shaw, Sheridan, Beckett and Behan, the curtain never falls on theatrical tradition.

Of course, nobody could ever guarantee you a suntan in Ireland, but the beauty of the island, and the warmth of the people will certainly burn a place in your heart.

A Brief History

As with all the great, timeless sagas, the story of Ireland is propelled on waves of tragedy, challenge and adventure. For the Irish of today, the ancient legends are as close as yesterday, historic crises as topical as this morning's headlines.

Relics from the Stone Age lead to the general conclusion that Ireland has been inhabited for at least 8,000 years. The first settlers here may well have even travelled on foot from Scandinavia to Scotland – England was linked at that time to northern Europe by land – then across what was a narrow sea gap to Ireland.

Sometimes referred to as Druid's Alter, Dolmons, such as these at Carrowmore, are a form of megalithic tomb.

During the later phase of the Stone Age, the inhabitants settled down as farmers. Tombs and temples from this period can be found in many parts of the country, usually in the middle of somebody's pasture. Some of the monuments are merely stone tripods; others, though, are as sophisticated as neolithic passage-graves, built on principles of astronomical alignment, containing strange engravings in spiral and zigzag patterns that had meaning for their creators.

Although new settlers and contacts with Europe brought along Bronze Age skills, Ireland still lagged behind the Continent in the next big revolution – the Iron Age. This technology finally reached the island during the last years of the pre-Christian era, brought in by tribes who originated in central Europe. Fighters truly worthy of legend, the language they spoke was Celtic.

The Roman legions which rolled across western Europe stopped short at the Irish Sea. This helps to explain why the Irish are so different: they developed their own way of life independently during the formative centuries of the great Roman Empire. Though Irish society was hopelessly decentralized – the sparse population widely dispersed under the sway of scores of bickering mini-kingdoms – a single culture did develop. Druids and poets told legends in a common language: one that was clearly recognizable as the Irish version of Gaelic.

St Patrick's Day

From time to time, the Celts staged raids on Roman Britain for booty and slaves. During one 5th-century raid, the tough Irish commandos rounded up a large number of captives to ease the manpower shortage. One of these 'immigrants', a 16-year-old boy, was later to become the national saint.

After a few years spent as a simple shepherd, he escaped to Gaul, heard the call of his life's mission, became a monk and finally returned to Ireland in order to convert heathens to Christianity.

St Patrick's crusade was a unique triumph – for Ireland is the only Western European country where the surrender of the pagans was achieved without a single Christian being martyred.

One of St Patrick's great innovations was the system of monasteries around which all church activities centred. This was suited to life in Ireland,

The perfect Round Tower, and Declan's Monastery (above) in the seaside town of Ardmore.

13

a rural and skimpily populated island with its diverse power blocs. While the rest of Europe crawled on through the Dark Ages, the flame of Western culture was kept alight in Irish monasteries. The monks of the 'island of saints and scholars' dutifully copied manuscripts from civilization; some of the books were so beautiful that they qualify as major works of art. The early Irish church leaders also founded an active missionary tradition.

The first great Irishman to propagate the faith beyond the sea was Colmcille, a scholarly poet of the 6th century who founded the Iona Monastery, near the coast of Scotland, and converted the Picts to Christianity. Young Colmcille, or St Columba, was succeeded by St Columbanus, whose long odyssey took in not only the whole of France, but also Switzerland, Austria and Italy as well. At this time, scholarly minds from different regions of Europe converged on the island in order to participate in its diverse and active religious and intellectual life.

The Vikings

At the turn of the 9th century, the security of Irish society was imperilled by tough and hardy intruders from the north. Well-armed warriors sailed in from Scandinavia aboard sleek boats in search of booty. The Irish monasteries holding their relics and treasures were easy targets for the Vikings. Their shallow-draught ships moved in and attacked virtually at will all around the Irish coast and up rivers as well.

The danger and uncertainty of the era inspired the design of multi-storey 'round towers'. Dozens of these combination watch-towers, belfries, store-houses and escape-hatches are still standing. In most of them the entrance was built high above ground level so the ladder could be hauled up at the first glimpse of a Norse sail.

Soon the sea-traffic became constructive, with the Vikings adding trading colonies around the coast. It was the Vikings who founded the first towns on the rural island – Dublin, Waterford and Limerick.

The Irish learned sailing, weaponry and metal-working from the Norse, but this did nothing to help the fact that their presence always rankled. Finally the natives ousted the Vikings, with the final struggle in the year 1014 at the Battle of Clontarf, when the High King of Ireland, Brian Boru, took on the tough Norse as well as their Irish allies. Boru was killed, but not before he had defeated the Vikings.

Cherchez La Femme

Behind the next invasion of Ireland lay many motivations, including jealousy. This tale begins in 1152, when the wife of Tiernan O'Rourke, one of the Irish warrior-kings, was carried off by a rival, Dermot MacMurrough of Leinster. It is alleged that the lady was a willing victim – in fact possibly even the instigator, but whichever the case, O'Rourke got his queen back a few months later.

However, being the kind of man he was, he wasn't about to forgive and forget.

O'Rourke and his allies put so much military pressure on King Dermot that in 1166 he fled first to England and then France. Dermot then shaped an alliance with a powerful Norman nobleman, the Earl of Pembroke. The Earl, known as Strongbow, agreed to lead an army to sweep Dermot back to power. The other half of the bargain struck was that the Earl would be given the hand of Dermot's daughter, and the right to succeed him to the Leinster throne. In the event, the hardy Normans – the élite of Europe's warriors – won the Battle of Waterford in 1169, and even before the raging flames of the battle had been extinguished, Strongbow married his heart's desire, the princess, in Waterford's grand cathedral.

In further engagements, the Norman war machine stunned and swiftly defeated the Norse and Irish forces. Indeed things were going so well for Strongbow that his overlord, King Henry of England, arrived on the scene in 1171 to assert his sovereignty.

15

Gael and Pale

The protracted Anglo-Norman occupation inevitably brought with it profound and long-lasting changes. Towns, churches and castles were built, and institutions for feudal government were created. Ireland was never totally conquered, however: the Irish identity was undiluted, and resistance and resentment persisted.

For the colonial rulers, the challenge of revolt was less serious than the danger of total cultural assimilation.

With the settlers adopting the ways of the natives, rather than the other way round, an attempt to enforce a form of apartheid was launched with the Statutes of Kilkenny (in 1366) introduced in order to forbid inter-marriage and ban the Gaelic language. English was spoken only in the Pale, that area around Dublin where the occupation forces were in command.

English control of Ireland was not actually consolidated until the grand House of Tudor turned its attention to Ireland, making it a training ground for the empire. King Henry VIII was the first English monarch to adopt the new title 'King of Ireland'. Following his break with Rome, he attempted to introduce the Reformation to Ireland as well as England, but the new religion only had real influence in the Pale and in the large provincial towns under

The pipes are one of the many instruments on which Irish music has been played for centuries.

English control, but in the rest of Ireland, the monasteries and the Catholicism they sought to nurture carried on as before, and so did the Irish language.

In the middle of the 16th century, the implementation of the so-called plantation policy pointed the way to large-scale redistribution of wealth as well as to the complete suppression of Catholicism. Desirable farm land was quickly confiscated from Catholics and given to Protestant settlers.

The hard Tudor conquest of Ireland ultimately required plenty of well-organised military armed force, and during the reign of Queen Elizabeth I, two major revolts had to be stopped. Throughout, the most unyielding resistance was in the city of Ulster. The Ulster chiefs, led by Hugh O'Neill, tried one last ploy – alliance with Queen Elizabeth's bitterest enemy, Spain. In the year 1601 a Spanish mini-armada sailed into the southern port of Kinsale. The English defeated the invaders as well as the Ulstermen who attempted to join them; but O'Neill, along with the leading Ulster aristocrats, soon abandoned their land for European exile. But the 'plantation' programme went on in fits and starts. Most of the land of the north was swiftly confiscated and 'planted' with thousands of Scots and English people, who made the city of Ulster forever different. After 1654, Catholics were only allowed to hold land to the west of the River Shannon, much of it scarcely habitable. 'To Hell or Connaught' was the slogan used to express the alternatives for the dispossessed.

Religious War

Events in England had their most violent repercussions in the mid-17th century. Oliver Cromwell arrived in Dublin soon after Charles I was executed, and supervised a campaign against those who had supported the king, in which the towns of Drogheda and Wexford were special targets for destruction. By the time Cromwell left Ireland in 1650, the backbone of resistance had been broken. **17**

Ireland again became a hard battleground when William of Orange, a Protestant, and now a culturally significant figure in English history, challenged his father-in-law, the Catholic James II, over the succession to the British throne. From his exile in France, James sailed to Ireland in order to mobilize his allies. William promptly came over from England for the showdown in July 1690, which is known as the Battle of the Boyne.

The Orangemen, aided by troops from several Protestant countries, vastly outnumbered the combined Irish and French forces commanded by James. As momentous battles go, it set no records either for scope nor for tactical innovation. Nor did it end the war as the losers fled to regroup. William of Orange was the winner of the Battle of the Boyne, and today its anniversary is celebrated with fervour by Protestants in Northern Ireland.

When the war finally ended with the Treaty of Limerick in 1691, the religious rights of Catholics were guaranteed. It comes as no surprise that the all-Protestant Irish parliament soon passed a series of 'Penal Laws' to keep all positions of power and influence well out of reach of the Catholic majority.

Revolutionary Ideas

The colonists' victory in the American Revolution sparked off daring and new thinking in Ireland. Agitation for greater freedom and tolerance was led by Henry Grattan, a Protestant of aristocratic heritage, who staunchly defended the rights of all Irishmen in the House of Commons in London. Some restrictions were eased a little and so Ireland won a limited measure of autonomy.

Further pressure in this field came from the Irish Protestant, Theobald Wolfe Tone, a young lawyer campaigning for parliamentary reform and abolition of the anti-Catholic laws.

A triumphant, garlanded figure-head guards the high walls of a typical Irish building.

British government tried to ban Wolfe Tone's supporters, the United Irishmen – but in 1793 Catholics won the vote as well as other concessions for which he fought.

Five years later, with the United Irishmen in rebellion, a French squadron came to their aid off the coast of Donegal and was swiftly intercepted by the British naval forces.

Wolfe Tone was captured on board the flagship of the fleet; he was wearing the uniform of a French officer. Convicted of treason, he committed suicide before his sentence could be carried out.

In 1801 the Irish parliament was abolished. It voted itself out of business after approving the Act of Union which established the United Kingdom of Great Britain and Ireland. All Irish politicians would now sit with MPs at Westminster, and thus the Mother of Parliaments was to govern Ireland from afar. The idea behind this was for the economic and political destinies of the two islands to become inseparable, but Irish nationalism has never really faded away.

A leading opponent of the act was one Daniel O'Connell, one of the first Catholics ever to gain admission to the Irish Bar. In 1823 he founded the Catholic Association, a mass-movement working for emancipation. He won a landslide victory only five years later in a by-election for the House of Commons, but as a Catholic he was paradoxically legally forbidden to take his seat. To quench more conflict, Parliament swiftly passed the Emancipation Act (1829), in which the most discriminative laws were removed. Subsequently, O'Connell tried to gain the repeal of the Act of Union, and although he failed, he is today remembered in Ireland as 'The Liberator'.

Starvation and Emigration

One of the worst disasters of 19th-century Europe was the great Irish famine.

The first hint of a problem was in September 1845, when the disease potato blight was discovered on farms in southeast Ireland. The British government immediately set up an investigation, but the outbreak was not diagnosed correctly. The next crop was a disaster nationwide and the staple food of the Irish peasant totally disappeared. Cruel winter weather and an inevitable outbreak of disease added to the horror of starvation.

The survivors stampeded to flee the stricken land aboard creaking 'coffin ships'. Pitiful Irish refugees swamped towns such as Liverpool, Halifax, Boston and New York. The toll of the famine is estimated to have reduced the population of Ireland by two million: half of them died, and the rest emigrated. It took another century before the constant decline in the population figures was redressed, and the flow of emigrants was stemmed.

Emigrants were among the founders of the Irish Republican Brotherhood – the Fenian movement – a broadly-based secret organization dedicated to overthrowing British rule. An IRB uprising in 1867 was crushed, but the survivors regrouped and planned a very successful revolt. They had to wait some 49 years for their big chance.

In the last part of the 19th century, two different Irishmen led a major campaign to return the land to the peasants. The first of these, Michael Davitt, was the founder of the Land League. He was a revolutionary who had a normal, working-class background, and one arm. The other, Charles Stewart Parnell, who became the Land League's president, was a Member of Parliament of the Protestant upper class.

Together they declared the famous 'land war' of 1879-82, in which great masses of the people became involved. The struggle finally brought down the landlord structure. In one incident, a County Mayo land agent just refused to grant his co-operation to the reformers. The Land League cut him off from the rest of the world so well that the name of the man, Charles Boycott, passed into English as the common word for an organized snub.

Frustration and Revolt

At the end of the 19th century a series of frustrations beset the forces for Irish autonomy or home rule. Charles Parnell, the shining hope of the Irish cause, lost influence once he was convicted of adultery said to have been committed with the wife of a fellow Member **21** of Parliament. New home rule legislation was pushed through the Commons, but it was rejected in the Lords.

Nationalist sentiment was encouraged, as distinct as the Gaelic Athletic Association and the Gaelic League (which defends Irish against its rapid decline). In 1905 a number of nationalist groups were consolidated in a new movement called Sinn Fein (which is Irish for 'ourselves').

Legislation for home rule looked more abstract than ever when Britain entered World War I, and so activists decided that the time would never be more apt for an uprising.

The Easter Rising of 1916 saw rebels seize the General Post Office in Dublin, and in a symbolic gesture they proclaimed it as a new government for the Irish Republic. The authorities soon crushed this move, which had in any case lacked general support, but the fast and pitiless repression which sent the leaders to the firing squad shocked the people and prepared the way for the war of independence.

At the next general election the nationalist Sinn Fein, now led by Eamon de Valera, won by a landslide. De Valera, born in New York City of an Irish mother and a Spanish father, had been a commander during the Easter Rising.

Two Irelands

The newly-elected Sinn Fein parliamentarians refused to fill their posts in the Commons in London, but instead set themselves up in Dublin as Dail Eireann, the new parliament of Ireland.

There followed more than two years of guerrilla warfare and reprisals by the government until finally the crisis was cooled by the partition of Ireland which took place in December 1921. Under it, six counties of the north, where the majority of the population was Protestant and opposed to rule from Dublin, remained part of the United Kingdom. The other 26 counties were of Catholic majority, and became the Irish Free State, a dominion within the British Empire.

Fervant republicans rejected the partition and partial links with Britain, and unleashed a civil war commonly known as 'The Troubles' which shook the brand new state. Among the many casualties of nearly a year's hard fighting was one Michael Collins, the commander of the provisional government's armed forces and a legendary independence fighter; he was killed in an ambush in August 1922.

Eire, the new country, progressively loosened ties with Britain, with the most conclusive demonstration being Ireland's neutrality in World War I. After the war, the new Republic was admitted to the UN and so undertook a new, international role, providing troops for peace-keeping operations.

When Britain and Ireland joined the EEC (now the European Union), hopes bloomed that both countries might be able to work more closely together; but the deadly mutual problem which has plagued their history over the war-torn passage of time – the Northern Ireland question – has eluded

*V*ictorian mail-boxes bring to mind Ireland's colourful past.

solution. Years of violence and intransigence have shown no way out of the crisis, even the idea of talks has been controversial, although the Downing Street Declaration in 1994 is a strong attempt at a solution. Meanwhile, it seems that the roots of this conflict go too deep into the island's history. **23**

Where to Go

You can't see it all. Ireland's geographic surface area may be modest, but it contains too many worthwhile sights to see in a single vacation. It would take three weeks simply to try out all the different day-trips run by CIE, the national Irish transport company. Big decisions have to be made on what to see and they will all depend on how much time you have, what you prefer to see, and on how you're travelling.

The best way to see Ireland is by car, through various fly-drive package deals or coach tours as an alternative. You can see a large proportion of Ireland using public transport, although apart from the main routes, the bus schedules tend to be designed more for country folk than tourists.

Ancient Ireland was divided into four provinces: Leinster (including Dublin); Munster in the south west; the rugged grandeur of westernmost Connacht; and to the north Ulster, with its striking coastline.

This book covers the high-spots of Ireland roughly in that order, starting in Dublin and proceeding more or less clockwise. We cannot describe all the sights – or even all the counties, but wherever you go, you'll enjoy Ireland more at an Irish pace.

Dublin

Pop. 915,000
(Greater Dublin)
The capital of Ireland is a very European city with low-profile buildings, many of them truly outstanding examples of 18th-century architecture, as well as the birthplace and inspiration of great authors.

Dublin is pervaded by contrasting moods which affect even transient visitors: from its noble avenues and intimate side-streets to chic shopping and old smoky pubs, there are also museums, colleges and plenty of sports. In this melting pot of old and new, traditional lace still masks modern windows and policemen on bicycles report in by lapel radio.

The city's name comes from the Irish *Dubhlinn*, meaning 'a dark pool', and a much older Gaelic name on buses and signs – *Baile Atha Cliath*, 'the town of the hurdle ford' – explains why Dublin was originally settled: it was a place to ford the River Liffey.

The river, with its tranquil canals and entrance to the Irish Sea nearby all contribute to the atmosphere. Seagulls frequent the centre of town, as do the ghosts of marauding Vikings, Normans, Viceroys .... as well as Leopold and Molly Bloom, late of Eccles Street.

The Must See Sights

Achill Island cliffs and beaches, Co. Mayo (see p.97)

Aran Islands (see p.94)

Ben Bulben mountain and WB Yeats' grave, Co. Sligo (see p.98)

Burren, Co. Clare (lunar landscape, many unique species of flora – see p.88)

Dingle peninsula (see p.82)

Dublin's 18th-century Georgian district (see p.26)

Giant's Causeway, Co. Antrim (see p.100)

Glendalough Mountains (see p.45)

Mourne Mountains (see p.101)

Newgrange prehistoric site, Co. Meath (see p.40)

Phoenix Park, Dublin (see p.37)

Ring of Kerry drive (see p.64)

Rock of Cashel, Co. Tipperary (see p.52)

Twelve Bens mountains, Co. Galway (see p.94)

West Cork (see p.62)

O'CONNELL STREET TO ST STEPHEN'S GREEN

The main street in Dublin is **O'Connell Street**, worthy of a major capital, and a lasting monument to the Wide Street Commissioners of the 1900s. Measuring 150ft (46m) across, it is straight as the morals of Father Theobald Mathew, the deeply admired 19th-century priest known as the Apostle of Temperance, who is commemorated in one of the four monuments down the middle of the road. There used to be five, but as a strong anti-British gesture in 1966, anonymous citizens planned a removal of Nelson Pillar, erected in 1808. Some Dubliners still admire the daring and panache of the crew that blew it up in the middle of the night.

The most famous landmark on O'Connell Street is the **General Post Office**, which has a significance far greater than its postal predominance. The GPO was the command post of the 1916 Easter Rising and was badly damaged in the fighting. A plaque on the front of the building, in Irish and English, and the statue inside mark the historic event.

To the south, just opposite O'Connell Bridge, is the large and complex monument hon-

The River Liffey winds its way through Dublin – a watery playground for locals and visitors.

26

ouring 'The Liberator', Daniel O'Connell (1775-1847), and after whom both the street and bridge are named.

From the bridge, almost as wide as it is long, you can look up and down the **River Liffey** and along the embankments. To the east, beyond the skyscraper-style headquarters of the Irish trade unions, rises the copper dome of the majestic

18th-century **Custom House**. Like many buildings along the River Liffey, it was all but destroyed in the civil war fighting of 1921, but has now been magnificently restored to its present gleaming white.

Some of the most interesting old buildings, including a few disused churches, are now occupied by banks, but it may come as a surprise to learn that

the momentous white building facing College Green on the south side of the River Liffey is in fact the headquarters of the **Bank of Ireland** company. It was built in the 18th century as a home for parliament, but when parliament was abruptly abolished by the Act of Union in 1800 (see p.20), the bank moved in. The grand portico has 22 Ionic columns.

Behind the railings at the entrance to **Trinity College** are the statues of two famous alumni – philosopher Edmund Burke and playwright Oliver Goldsmith. Founded by Queen Elizabeth I in 1592, Trinity is a timeless enclave of calm and scholarship in the middle of this bustling city. For centuries it was seen as an exclusively Protestant institution, and as recently as 1956 the Catholic church forbade its students to attend Trinity 'under pain of mortal sin'. Today, TCD, as it is called, is integrated.

Most of the campus forms a monument to the good taste of the 18th century, and visitors enjoy cobbled walks amongst **28** trimmed lawns, fine old trees,

statues and stone buildings. (Appropriately, the movie *Educating Rita* was filmed here.) The greatest treasures are in the vaulted Long Room in the **Old Library**, where double-decker shelving holds thousands of books published prior to 1800, and priceless early manuscripts are displayed in glass cases.

In the adjacent Colannades Gallery queues of students and tourists reverently wait for a look at the **Book of Kells**. This 340-page parchment wonder, hand-written and illustrated by monks during the 9th century, contains a Latin version of the New Testament. The beauty of the script, the illumination (the deciration of initial letters and words) and the bright abstract designs – above all the saintly portraits – constitute the most wonderful treasure to survive from Ireland's Golden Age. The vellum leaves are turned every day to protect them from the light and to give visitors a chance to come back for more.

Examples of Europe's finest Georgian houses can be seen facing **Merrion Square**, once the proposed site for a Catholic cathedral and now a park. The discreet, smart brick houses have those Dublin doorways which are flanked by tall columns and topped by fanlights. No two are alike. In a complex of formal buildings on the west side of the square, stands the city's largest 18th-century mansion, home of the Duke of Leinster. Today **Leinster House** is the seat of the Irish parliament, which consists of the Senate (*Seanad*) and the Chamber of Deputies (the *Dail*, which is pronounced 'doyle').

Standing at the entrance to the **National Gallery** you will see a statue of George Bernard Shaw, famous and respected Dubliner, known locally as a benefactor of the institution.

*D*ublin's main street is named in honour of Daniel O'Connell, who won Catholic emancipation for Ireland.

29

A Way with Words

Story-telling comes naturally to the Irish. Ireland's rich literary heritage is brought to life in the Dublin Writers Museum (18-19 Parnell Square North), where fixed displays are complemented with lectures, readings and talks. There is also a Living Writers Centre, where visiting writers are welcome, and a children's section, where story-times are held.

Here are some of Ireland's greatest authors.

Jonathan Swift (1667-1745), a satirist and the dean of St Patrick's Cathedral. Writing was only a part-time job for the romantic clergyman best remembered for *Gulliver's Travels*.

Oliver Goldsmith (c. 1728-74) studied medicine, then entered the London circle of Dr Samuel Johnson. He wrote the novel *The Vicar of Wakefield*, the play *She Stoops to Conquer* and the poem *The Deserted Village*.

Oscar Wilde (1854-1900). His haunting, original novel, *The Picture of Dorian Gray*, was followed by witty comedies like *The Importance of Being Earnest*. Imprisoned on a charge of homosexual conduct, he wrote *The Ballad of Reading Gaol*.

George Bernard Shaw (1856-1950), Dublin-born, spent most of his life in England. *Arms and the Man*, *Man and Superman* and *Pygmalion* made him the greatest dramatist of the age. Shaw was also an inveterate controversialist.

William Butler Yeats (1865-1939), like Shaw, won the Nobel prize. His poems sang the glories of Ireland. A founder of the Abbey Theatre and senator of the young Irish Free State.

Sean O'Casey (1880-1964), wrote tragi-comedy – *The Shadow of a Gunman*, *Juno and the Paycock* and *The Plough and the Stars*. His later plays were less successful.

James Joyce (1882-1941) re-created Dublin in his imagination from European exile. *Ulysses*, his revolutionary stream-of-consciousness novel in a Homeric framework, was banned in Ireland (and elsewhere) during his lifetime.

*T*he Natural History Museum in Merrion Street is part of the National Museum of Ireland.

In the **National Gallery** some 2,000 works of art are displayed, but 6,000 more are held in reserve. Irish artists receive priority, but other nationalities are also well represented such as Dutch, English, Flemish, French, Italian and Spanish masters. Among those on display are, in chronological order: Fra Angelico, Rubens, Rembrandt, Canaletto, Gainsborough and Goya. In addition, rounding off what is a prize collection of medieval religious art, is the gallery's treasured and most recent acquisition: two glorious frescoes dating from the 11th or 12th century, delicately lifted from the walls of the Chapel of St-Pierre-de-Campublic in Beaucaire, France.

The main entrance to the **National Museum**, an important Dublin institution, is reached from Kildare Street.

The museum's collection of Irish antiquities contains several surprises, from old skeletons and tools to exquisite gold ornaments of the Bronze Age. The most famous items on display include the 8th-century Ardagh Chalice, the delicate Tara Brooch from the same era and the Shrine of St Patrick's Bell (dating from the 12th century). You can also see ancient Ogham stones complete with inscriptions in what appears to be a childish method of encoding Latin.

If you don't have time to make a full tour of churchyards and far-off monasteries, you can admire many replicas **31** of the greatest carved stone crosses from early centuries of Christian Ireland.

The south-eastern part of central Dublin is handsomely and unusually well endowed with breathing space, thanks to a number of pleasant squares and parks. The biggest of these – and possibly the biggest city square in Europe – is the famous **St Stephen's Green**.

During the 18th century the square was almost completely surrounded by elegant town houses, some surviving today,

though many conservationists despair at the rapidly declining number. Inside the square is a perfectly delightful park with pretty flower gardens and a man-made lake inhabited by waterfowl. Among the many sculptures and monuments in varied styles there is also a memorial to the poet and playwright WB Yeats by Henry Moore. Nearby is also a bust to commemorate Yeats' friend who is today seen as a historic figure, the Countess Constance Markievicz, who defended the square during the 1916 insurrection, and who was the first woman elected to the British House of Commons.

Another statue honours the man who paid for landscaping the square: Lord Ardilaun, son of the founder of the Guinness brewery. Some thirsty sightseers might be inspired to find a nearby pub and raise a toast to the stout-hearted benefactor.

Of course there are plenty of peaceful places even in the bustling city of Dublin.

MEDIEVAL DUBLIN

Dublin Castle was begun in the 13th century, set on a hill high above the original Viking settlement on the south bank of the River Liffey. It was rebuilt during the 18th century, which explains why it no longer looks like a medieval castle. Over the years it has served as a seat of government, as a prison, a courthouse, and occasionally as a fortress under siege – most recently in 1916. Many visiting heads of state have been fêted in the lavish State Apartments, which were once the grand residence of the British Viceroy.

Around the corner from the castle stands the **City Hall** (in former times the Royal Exchange). Built during the late 18th century in solid, classical style, it contains an interesting collection of royal charters and municipal regalia

Dublin has not one but two noteworthy cathedrals to offer, and although it is the official capital of what is a predominantly Catholic country, both of the cathedrals belong to the Protestant Church of Ireland. The reason for two cathedrals is easily explained if you have the time to sift through the various historic, 12th-century political and religious rivalries which had an effect here.

In any case, **Christ Church** cathedral is the older of the two, dating from 1038. One unusual architectural touch is the covered pedestrian bridge over Winetavern Street, which links the church and its synod house. This was built during the Victorian era, but doesn't spoil the overall mood. Otherwise, Christ Church cathedral boasts Romanesque, as well as Early English and fine neo-Gothic elements.

The crypt, which runs under the full length of the church, rather like a vast wine-cellar, is a surviving remnant from the 12th century, during which the cathedral was expanded by Strongbow (see p.15), whose mortal remains lie buried here. Although it has been regarded as authentic for many decades, modern scholars are in heated debate about the authenticity of the Strongbow tomb. **33**

St Audeon's Church in Dublin was founded by Normans during the 12th century.

You can see the fine statue of a recumbent cross-legged knight in full armour in the southern aisle

If you would like to delve more deeply into Irish history, you could visit novel Dublinia, which is in the former synod **34** hall of the cathedral. This is a brand new, impressive multimedia heritage centre depicting how Dubliners lived in the medieval city, offering Viking artefacts and a closing audiovisual show.

A short walk south from Christ Church cathedral leads to Dublin's newer and larger cathedral, **St Patrick's**, which is dedicated to Ireland's national saint. It is said that St Patrick himself baptized 5th-century converts at a well on this very site; indeed a stone slab which was used for covering the well can be found in the north west of the cathedral. This church was consecrated in 1192, but the present architectural structure dates mostly from the 13th and 14th centuries. The cathedral is known for its association with the writer Jonathan Swift, the famous crusading satirist, who was appointed dean in 1713, and served until his death in 1745. Many Swiftian relics can be seen in a corner of the north transept, and a simple brass plate in the floor near the entrance marks his grave. Next to this you can see the tomb of the mysterious Stella, one of the two great loves of his life. Above the lintel of the robing room you can read his own bitter epitaph, written in Latin: 'Savage indignation can no longer gnaw his heart. Go, traveller, and imitate, if you can, this earnest and dedicated defender of liberty.'

The talented choirboys of St Patrick's Cathedral lift up their voices – and the hearts of listeners – at the services given every day of the week except on Saturdays.

A joint choir formed from both cathedrals was the first to sing Handel's *Messiah* when the composer was in Dublin in 1742. A copy from the year 1799 can be seen in Marsh's Library, Ireland's first public library, founded in 1701.

Temple Bar is a city area which runs from Westmoreland Street to Christ Church Cathedral. With its 18th and 19th century architecture, major developments are aimed at turning the area into the arts and crafts quarter of Dublin. The Irish Film Centre, as well as other attractions, including a Viking Museum, will have emerged by the time work is finished in 1996. Temple Bar is a useful area to consider for dining out.

THE NORTH BANK

The most impressive building located on the north bank of the Liffey is the domed home of the **Four Courts** (originally the Chancery, Common Pleas, Exchequer and King's Bench). This is the magnificent work of James Gandon, the respect- **35** ed 18th century, English-born architect who also designed Dublin's Custom House. The courthouse was quite seriously damaged by the consistent and prolonged shelling during the 1922 civil war. After lengthy reconstruction, however, it was restored to its original use, and justice continues to be dispensed in the neo-classic Four Courts. Carrying on the tradition which was introduced by the British, Irish lawyers in action today wear handsome wigs and gowns.

St Michan's Church, just around the corner in Church Street, was founded in 1095 and has in fact been completely rebuilt on several occasions since then. Among the curiosities you can see is a unusual, so-called 'Penitent's Pew', in which sinners had to sit and confess their sins aloud to the whole congregation.

In the vaults, wood coffins and mummies can be seen in a remarkably healthy state of preservation. Some of them have been here for over 200 years; saved from certain deterioration by the dry air preva-

lent in the rooms of the crypt or perhaps by its high methane content. It's all a bit spooky.

The last imposing official building to be designed by the architect James Gandon was the **King's Inns**, which houses the headquarters of the Irish legal profession. It contains an important law library and a magnificent dining hall where the grandest portraits of many judges decorate the walls.

On the north side of Parnell Square is Charlemont House, one of Dublin's most attractive 18th-century mansions, which is now the **Municipal Gallery of Modern Art**. It includes magnificent pieces from the superb collection of Sir Hugh Lane. Sadly he was drowned in the *Luisitania* disaster of 1915, provoking a long legal struggle over custody of his paintings. For 20 years his pictures shuttled back and forth between Dublin and London, but the latest agreement assures the Municipal Gallery three-quarters of the contested legacy, including works by Corot, Courbet, Manet, Monet and Rousseau.

BEYOND THE CENTRE

The **Phoenix Park** provides Dubliners with nearly 3 square miles (8sq km) of beautiful parkland. It's huge monument is an obelisk honouring the Duke of Wellington, who was born in Ireland, but was later to quip that although a man may be born in a stable, that wouldn't make him a horse. Among the numerous buildings discreetly located in the park are the residence of the President of Ireland (*Arasan Uachtarain*), and the Ashtown Castle Heritage Centre, which details the history of the park and its flora and fauna.

The Four Courts on the banks of the River Liffey, designed by James Gandon, has been restored to its original splendour.

On the north-east side of Phoenix Park, Dublin **zoo** provides education and diversion; it is noted for breeding lion cubs in captivity.

In Kilmainham on the South Circular Road, a stone tower-gate guards the grounds of the **Royal Hospital**, which as the city's main 17th-century building, was a home for army pensioners. Now it is the **Irish Museum of Modern Art**.

The ugly and forbidding **Kilmainham Jail** has been restored as if it were a work of art. The prisoners who lived and died within its walls include many of the heroes of Irish nationalism. The jail is open daily for visitors and the central cell block shows a few exhibits from Ireland's stormy, revolutionary history.

Jails make unlikely tourist attractions, as does a factory. Nevertheless, many make their way to the biggest enterprise, the **Guinness Brewery** based at St James' Gate. The firm has been on this site since 1759, and its dark, full-bodied stout is known far and wide. Visitors are shown a film about the manufacturing process and invited to sample the finished product. There's also a gallery of modern art.

In the Ballsbridge district of south-east Dublin you can find the spacious grounds of the **Royal Dublin Society** (RDS). A golden and green privet hedge surrounds the fields in which one of the greatest horse shows in the world is held (in August). The RDS complex is also used for agricultural and industrial exhibitions, as well as conferences and concerts.

This area, rich in parkland and large residences, boasts many foreign embassies, a fair number of them in Ailesbury Road. Just around the corner is the **Chester Beatty Library and Gallery of Oriental Art**. Its collection is well-known for priceless manuscripts and miniatures from the East: jade books from China, early Arabic tomes on geography and astronomy, and a sampling of Korans. The collector and donor behind all this was Sir Alfred Chester Beatty (1875-1968), an American who retired to Ireland.

Dublin Daytrips

In the north-eastern part of the Bay, **Howth peninsula** makes an appealing starting point for those wishing to venture out of Dublin. From the vantage point of the 560ft (170m) Hill of Howth, you can survey the bay and the open sea. Howth Harbour, on the north side of the peninsula, is a fishing port as well as a haven for pleasure boats. From here you can see and visit Ireland's Eye, an islet a mile offshore popular with birds and bird-watchers.

Malahide, a small resort town, is perhaps best known for its **castle**, a two-turreted medieval pile with a lived-in look. The spirit of the Talbot family, who resided here for 791 years, still pervades – not only with the portraits on the walls, but even the colour of the walls, 'Malahide orange'. It is a tint found only here. Part of the National Portrait Collection is also here. Lawns surround the castle, bought by the Dublin County Council after the death of the last Lord Talbot in 1975.

The Fry Model Railway Museum is the largest model railway in Ireland and one of the largest in Europe. It shows transport in Ireland over the past 150 years, and all of it is electronically controlled.

Drogheda is an industrial township with a population of 24,000. It straddles the River Boyne near to where the 1690 battle took place in which King James II lost his chance to recover the English crown (see p18). This medieval city was surrounded by a wall with ten gates – you can still drive through the 13th-century **St Lawrence's Gate**, with its two towers standing as vigilantly as ever. In the town centre **St Peter's Church** has been dedicated to St Oliver Plunkett (1628-81), the Archbishop of Armagh, who was executed by the British in connection with an alleged Popish Plot. Several relics of the local saint are displayed in the church including the actual door of his cell at Newgate Prison and, most amazing of all, his head, which is embalmed and kept in a gold case in a side altar. **39**

Six miles to the north west is **Monasterboice** (St Buithe's Abbey), one of the numerous ancient Irish monastic settlements. Above it all stands the jagged top of what is thought to have been the tallest round tower in Ireland, 110ft (34m) high. Along with the remains of two ruined churches there are three important examples of early Christian high crosses. Many of the intricately carved figures portray New Testament subjects, others are abstract.

A high medieval gatehouse sternly guards the approach to **Mellifont Abbey**, Ireland's most important early Cistercian monastery. The buildings include the remains of a large church and the Lavabo, which is a most unusual and graceful octagonal building of which only four sides remain today. Like most other abandoned monastic institutions, Mellifont is set in peaceful and verdant country.

Newgrange, a massive Neolithic tomb, looks like a man-made hilltop. It is an amazing feat of prehistoric engineering, and not least because of the narrow tunnel leading to the central shrine, which was posi-

tioned to let the sun shine in precisely on the shortest day of the year, 21 December. Newgrange, on the north bank of the Boyne, is considered one of Europe's best examples of a passage-grave. The 62ft (19m) tunnel is, incredibly, high and wide enough for a tourist to walk through at a crouch. At the end of it you can stand in the circular vault and look up at the imposing high ceiling and marvel at the incredible 4,000-year-old technique used in its construction.

There are intruiging carvings which can be seen in spiral, circular and diamond designs, and which decorate the stones in the inner sanctum, and at the entrance. Outside, a dozen large, upright stones, about one-third of those originally placed here, form a generous, protective circle around the mound.

Two further Neolithic tumuli were discovered nearby at

Ireland's Eye (left), is a tiny islet just off Howth (below), a fishing village with delightful views and invigorating walks.

two places called Knowth and Dowth, which suggests that this was regarded as a special place in prehistoric times.

The scribes and artists of the monastery at **Kells**, located in County Meath, are credited with producing the nation's most beautiful book, now on display at Trinity College in Dublin (see p.28). The town of Kells has grown up around the monastic settlement, and there is a fine Celtic cross standing at the main traffic intersection. Near the cemetery are several other high, stone crosses and a round tower, practically intact and almost 100ft (30m) high.

As its name indicates, **Trim** is a well-kept, tidy town. In fact, the terse English name is derived from the Irish *Baile Atha Trium*, which means 'the town of the Elder-Tree Ford'. The river in question is the Boyne, which adds greatly to the beauty of the area.

Trim claims it has Ireland's largest medieval **castle**, once a Norman stronghold. Vast it is, but time has left only the bare bones. The Dublin Gate in the south once contained a prison.

On the opposite side of the river, the Yellow Steeple is like a finger pointing upwards. It was part of an Augustinian abbey established in the 13th century; the tower was blown up deliberately to keep it out of the hands of Cromwell.

West of Dublin, landlocked **County Kildare** has some of the greenest pastures in all of Ireland. It's a great area for sports, but there is no shortage of historic sites amidst the rolling hills.

Maynooth, a pleasant town with a college history and the ruins of a 12th-century castle, is a training-ground for priests. Founded in 1795, St Patrick's College is seen as one of the foremost Catholic seminaries in the world.

On the edge of the village of Celbridge, **Castletown House** stands at the end of a very long avenue of trees. This stately home, in Palladian style, was erected in 1722 for the speaker of the Irish House of Commons, William Connolly, and has been restored and refurnished with 18th-century antiques and paintings.

*T*he sheltered harbour of Dun Laoghaire, on the southern shores of Dublin Bay, is an ideal location for yachting and sea angling.

A few miles from the house Connolly's widow ordered the construction of a monstrous obelisk. Known as Connolly's Folly, it was erected, with the best of intentions, to provide employment for local workers who were suffering the Great Famine of 1740.

The administrative centre of the county, Naas (the Irish *Nas na Ri*, means Assembly-Place of the Kings), has an important race-course. So does nearby Punchestown. The capital of horseracing and breeding is the **Curragh**, a prairie from Droichead Nua (New Bridge) all the way to Kildare Town, but it's still a shock to come upon a modern grandstand – site of the Irish Sweeps Derby – right in the middle of this endless plain.

Many of the winners of the world's big races were born at the **National Stud** at Tully. Here the thoroughbreds live in the equivalent of a first-class motel. Visitors are allowed in from Easter to October, and as a sort of side-show to the main event, there is an immaculate **Japanese Garden** adjoining the Stud. In the beginning of the 20th century, one Japanese gardener and 40 local men worked for four long years to transform an Irish bog into a little world of sheared shrubs, disciplined trees, a lotus pond and even a teahouse and red wooden bridge.

The town of **Kildare** is also remembered for the unusual double monastery (monks and nuns) founded there by the 5th-century St Brigid. Though the buildings were quite badly damaged by the Vikings and many other invaders, the shape of the 19th-century **cathedral** (Church of Ireland) features 13th-century elements. Nearby you can also inspect an ancient round tower still in very good shape, with stairs all the way to the summit.

The ruins of another ancient monastery are at the southern end of County Kildare, in the village of **Castledermot**. Only two beautifully carved crosses remain, and the portal of a church that could be as much as a thousand years old. The design of this ruin has been repeated in a new church just a few yards behind it.

Dun Laoghaire, just south of Dublin, is Ireland's leading yachting centre. The piers at the harbour are 1 mile (2km) long, leaving plenty of space between for the huge fleet of pleasure boats as well as the car ferry terminal. Construction of the harbour was seen as a great feat of 19th-century marine engineering – and it's still impressive. You can also visit the Maritime Museum, which features many exhibits relating to Ireland's maritime history. Dun Laoghaire, Dublin's largest suburb, is pronounced 'Dunleary'.

About a mile to the south at **Sandycove** is an 18th-century tower. James Joyce lived in it, and used this experience in the opening of his work *Ulysses*.

The Martello Tower (named after a town in Corsica) was part of a network of coastal defences erected to ward off an invasion by Napoleon, and has now been turned into a museum to Joyce. A second Martello Tower can be seen on Dalkey Island, the largest of a group of islands off Dalkey.

Just across the border in County Wicklow, the popular resort of **Bray** has a 1-mile (2km) sand-and-shingle beach backed by an esplanade. The Wicklow coast is mostly sandy and low-lying, and the interior of the county is known as the Garden of Ireland.

West of Bray, near the small village of Enniskerry, is the most majestic park you're ever likely to see. The grand estate of **Powerscourt** descends in disciplined terraces to a lake with a fountain in the middle. Taking in manifold acres of

The Forty Foot Hole in Sandycove was once a male bathers' preserve – now it's a favourite place for all to take a dip.

elegant, spectacular scenery, it has an 18th-century, 100-room mansion at its centre, which was unfortunately damaged in a fire in 1974. But all was not lost: the gardens, statues, gates and fountains are as beautiful as ever. The grounds are open from Easter to October and the Powerscourt Waterfall, several miles south of the house itself, may be visited all year round.

In the ruins of the ancient monastic city of **Glendalough** tombstones dating back hundreds of years alternate with more newly-covered graves.

*B*ray, with its magnificent headland, is one of Ireland's best known seaside resorts and perfect for exploring the surrounding countryside.

The original gateway to the settlement is still standing, the only one of its kind remaining in Ireland. Inside, on the right, a cross-inscribed stone may have marked the limit of the sanctuary granted to all those who took refuge within the monastery.

As you enter this site, which is located in a narrow, wooded valley, you suddenly stumble across the perfectly preserved historic **round tower**, a thousand years old. With its graceful, tapered shape and pert conical roof, it might easily be mistaken for a missile on a launch pad. This tower was the place to sit out any sieges; its doorway is built 11½ft (3.5m) above the ground – enough to discourage even Vikings from attempting an invasion.

The hermit St Kevin founded the monastery in the 6th century. He was inspired by the breathtaking scenery and its remoteness, and planned it as a small but contemplative institution. As its fame spread far and wide, Glendalough of the Seven Churches became an important monastic city, until in 1398 it was destroyed by Anglo-Normans. The ruins of the churches and buildings are particularly evocative, set as they are amid wild beauty.

In **Avondale**, you can visit the home of Charles Stewart Parnell, the great 19th century Irish leader, which has been restored in 1850s style. It is set in an area of verdant forest and woodland and makes an ideal destination for walkers. **Grand Russborough House**, near Blessington, is an 18th-century house in grand Palladian style.

Today it houses the Sir Alfred Beit art collection, and is beautifully and richly decorated, offering magnificent views across the ornamental lake towards the splendid Wicklow mountains.

The South East

Meteorologists confirm what everyone in Ireland has always believed: on average, over the whole year, the south east enjoys up to an hour more sunshine a day than other parts of Ireland. The better to see – and enjoy – the varied scenery, mountains and pastures, rivers, beautiful beaches and delightful, old towns.

Enniscorthy (the Irish *Inis Coirthe* means Rock Island) is a colourful inland port on the River Slaney, navigable from here to Wexford. High above the steep streets of the town, Vinegar Hill is a good vantage point for viewing the countryside. It was the scene of the last battle of the 1798 Rising, during which British General Lake overwhelmed the many Wexford rebels armed with pitchforks and pikes, dashing the struggle for independence.

Enniscorthy Castle, set in the centre of town, is a Norman keep which was rebuilt during the 16th century and was recently opened as a folk museum.

Wexford, the county seat, (15 miles/24km to the south) lays claim to a most historic past, having been one of the first Viking settlements in the land. In the 9th century it was called *Waesfjord*, meaning 'the harbour of the mudflats'. At low tide the original name still seems appropriate.

A few ancient monuments survive and are well signposted, with informative plaques explaining almost every legend of Wexford, which only adds to the interest of strolling around the back streets. The remaining medieval walls have all now been fully restored and a heritage centre opened.

The town of Enniscorthy is overlooked by Vinegar Hill, the famous site of the last battle of the 1798 Rising.

In addition, you can visit the **Irish National Heritage Park** in Ferrycarrig, north of town, to see a collection of lifesize replicas of ancient dwellings, burial sites, old monastic settlements and various types of fortification, from early Irish man up to the 12th century. Reminders of the area's seafaring past are on view at the Maritime Museum in the little, picturesque village of Kilmore Quay, about 15 miles south of Wexford. Housed in an old lightship, moored permanently in the harbour, the museum has numerous maritime artefacts to examine.

In the month of October, the Wexford Opera Festival offers a magnetic attraction for world performers and fans for even little-known works. The town is very proud of its year-round cultural pursuits.

South east of the town, the resort of **Rosslare** has a sight for sore eyes: a 6-mile (10km) crescent of beach. Beyond it is Rosslare Harbour, where car ferries arrive from and depart for Fishguard, Le Havre and Cherbourg.

Continuing this theme and just before turning inland, the tip of the **Hook peninsula** has a tall, 700-year-old lighthouse which warns mariners of the treacherous rocks, and signals the entrance to the Waterford harbour. But that's only half the story: a light has been kept burning at Hook Head for the last 1,500 years.

The Norse established ports such as Dublin and Wexford, but it somehow never occurred to them to found permanent settlements inland. It was the Normans who moved 20 miles (32km) up the estuary to build the town of **New Ross**, still an important inland port. In the middle of the 13th century, it was encircled by a strong and defensive wall.

The small, isolated hamlet of **Dunganstown**, near New Ross, was the birthplace of the great-grandfather of President John F Kennedy. A plaque marks the cottage from which he emigrated to Boston.

The assassinated president was much admired in Ireland, and you can often see his picture hanging like an icon on **49** living-room walls. A group of Irish-Americans and the Irish government later created the **John F Kennedy Park**, above Dunganstown. This appealing green memorial contains both mighty oak and chestnut trees, as well as shrubs, flowers and trimmed lawns. Visitors can follow the signposted walks or relax with a picnic.

Heading south west, over to County Waterford, you cross the historic frontier between the provinces of Leinster and Munster. As the largest in area of Ireland's four provinces, Munster boasts the cities of Cork and Limerick as well as thinly-inhabited farmland and romantic Atlantic shores.

With a population of 40,000 **Waterford** is a busy little port situated just 18 miles (29km) from the open sea. From the far side of the River Suir, its long quayside presents a pretty European image. Waterford's foundation can be traced back to the 9th century, but it did not gain its first charter until 1205, granted by King John of Magna Carta fame. The heritage centre in town has many

ancient relics from the Norse and Norman settlements of the city, and numerous municipal mementos are preserved inside **Reginald's Tower**, the city's most venerable building.

The walls of this massive circular fortification, 10ft (3m) thick and about 80ft (24m) tall, have survived many sieges since they went up in 1003, and the tower has had a chequered past, serving as a fortress, an arsenal and a mint, and as a barracks and prison. Now it contains the Waterford Civic Museum.

Among other attractions are the Garter Lane Arts Centre, perhaps the country's leading regional centre of its kind, as well as Celtworld at Tramore (see opposite), which is the seaside resort area of the city.

An elegant Georgian street, the Mall, begins at the Quay. Waterford City Hall, built during the 1780s, has many distinguished features including two small theatres and a Council Chamber elegantly and brightly illuminated by a splendid chandelier – made, logically, from Waterford glass.

The golden age of **Waterford glass** ran from 1783 to 1851. After a century's lapse, production was resumed, and the traditional processes can still be seen on guided tours of the factory, a few miles from Waterford town centre on the Cork road. It's best to check with the local tourist office before making a visit.

At **Tramore**, on the coast just below Waterford, you can experience **Celtworld**. This is a modern centre where audio-visual techniques are employed to great effect to relate the fascinating story of Ireland's ancient Celtic past, with several realistical large-scale models of famous old mythological figures.

At the western edge of the county, you can sample the Lismore Experience, another educative multi-media show. It tells the history of this small town, which was founded in the 7th century by St Carthage. Also, visit Ormond Castle in Carrick-on-Suir. This is a fine example of an old Elizabethan manor, now restored to its 16th century glory.

CASTLES AND KINGS

The counties of **Kilkenny** and **Tipperary** both feature stunning river valleys and the most imposing ruins from a regal past. Tipperary was once used as the home of the kings of Munster; Kilkenny has its own glory: it entered history as the ancient Kingdom of Ossory.

The main street in Clonmell, which means 'Honey Meadow', is awash with colourful buildings.

The main town in County Tipperary is called **Clonmel** (in Irish *Cluain Meala*, which means 'Honey Meadow'). A hamlet probably existed here before the Vikings. The town was walled in the 14th century, and parts of this can still be seen. The turreted West Gate was rebuilt in 1831 on the site of an original town gate.

The name of the township of **Cahir** is a short version of the Irish for 'Fortress of the Dun Abounding in Fish'. Its setting, on the River Suir, is both fetching and strategic. Upstream from the bridge, a family of swans bob above the weir; downstream a seemingly impregnable castle guards the crucial crossing. Built on the river's lovely islet – a site which has been fortified since the 3rd century – the present castle may date from the 15th century, or possibly earlier; the records are vague. It's in a fine state of restoration now and so is well worth a visit. Guided tours point out many military details, such as musket slits, a portcullis, and a cannonball embedded high in one of the

walls. While you're in Cahir, take a look at **Swiss Cottage**, an early 19th-century cottage ornée, in the bright style of the former Brighton Pavilion. It has been fully restored right down to the thatched roof and original French wallpaper.

In **Cashel** (County Tipperary), ruins majestically crown an imposing hilltop. On the **Rock of Cashel**, a 200ft (61m) high outcrop of limestone in the middle of a pasture, the kings of Munster established their headquarters from the 4th to the 12th century. When St Patrick visited in 450, he baptized King Aengus and his brothers. The hill was handed in 1101 to the ecclesiastical authorities, who built an Irish-Romanesque church on it.

Cormac's Chapel (consecrated in 1134) is different from all of the others because it was built by Irish monks who interpreted the different architectural styles they had studied in Europe. It features a steeply-pitched stone roof, rows of blank arches and two strangely positioned towers. Stone-carvings of beasts and abstract designs decorate the doorway and arches.

The chapel is dwarfed by the **cathedral** which abuts it. This structure, dating from the 13th-century, has both thick and well-preserved walls, but the roof collapsed during the 18th century. On the positive side, the resulting hole lets the sunlight stream in, helping to clarify the many architectural details, as well as the exquisite medieval stone-carvings.

St Patrick's Cross, inside the entrance, is one of the oldest crosses in Ireland, and it looks like it: the sculptures on both sides are very weather-beaten. Interestingly the cross rises up from the 'Coronation Stone', said to have been a sacrificial altar in pagan times.

With all these incomparable structures below, the perfect round tower looming above seems somehow to be a bit of an anticlimax.

The lively market town of **Thurles** has some claims to fame of its own. It was here in 1174 that the Irish forces inflicted a demoralizing defeat on the Anglo-Norman army led by Strongbow (see p.15). Seven hundred years later the town of Thurles was to be the birthplace of the Gaelic Athletic Association, now an amateur sports organization.

The most conspicuous landmark of the town, the Catholic Cathedral, is a 19th-century impression of the Romanesque style. The square bell tower, 125ft (38m) high, can be seen for miles around.

Four miles (6km) south of Thurles, on the west bank of the River Suir, **Holy Cross Abbey** boasts a 12th-century church which is still in daily use. The name of the church refers to a particle of the True Cross, enshrined in this old Cistercian Abbey over several centuries.

Construction of the church was started in Romanesque style, but the rebuilding and expansion programmes over the next centuries evolved into Gothic. The solid white walls, enhanced by window-tracery, reach up to a perfectly restored 15th-century ceiling. Experts acclaim the beautiful sedilia, and the triple-arched recess, **53**

*H*oly Cross Abbey (1168), was restored as part of the European Architectural Heritage Year in 1975 after standing roofless for over 200 years.

containing seats of honour, which is carved from jet black marble and decorated with ancient coats of arms. Another detail is the night stairs, down which the monks stumbled from their sleeping quarters at 2am to chant matins. One of the bells in the tower was cast in the early 13th century, making it Ireland's oldest.

Kilkenny has a colourful past and present. Among other surprises you will find, smack in the traffic-clogged centre **54** of this city, an enormous med-

ieval castle with acres of lawns – and a river to boot. This was the capital of the old Kingdom of Ossory, a small, feuding realm in pre-Norman Ireland.

Parliament, which convened here in 1366, passed the notorious but ineffectual Statute of Kilkenny with the aim of segregating the Irish from the Anglo-Normans; in those days intermarriage was seen as high treason. In the 17th century an independent Irish parliament met here for several years. Cromwell took the town in 1650, suffering heavy losses in the process but in the end capturing it.

The Irish *Cill Choinnigh* means St Canice's church and **St Canice's Cathedral**, built in the 13th century, is on the original site of the church, which gave the town its name.

Though Cromwell's rampaging troops badly damaged the building, it has since been restored to an admirable state. Medieval sculptures and monuments abound in this Protestant church. Alongside it is a round tower, part of the ancient church, so tall, slim and austere that it resembles a factory smokestack.

Kilkenny Castle was built in the 13th century to replace the original primitive fortress erected by Strongbow. The Butler family, one of the great Anglo-Norman dynasties, held the castle until 1935, but today it is owned by the Irish state. Three of the castle's original four towers remain. You will also find a brilliantly restored picture gallery on the upper floor of the north wing.

Kilkenny (with a population of 9,000) is packed with bright shops. In the High Street, the Tholsel, dating from the 18th century, has an eight-sided clock-tower like a lighthouse.

The Archaeological Society in Kilkenny runs a museum in **Rothe House**, a Tudor townhouse dating to 1594. The exhibits on display range from Stone Age tools unearthed locally to medieval relics.

Not far from Thomastown (in County Kilkenny) you can visit the partially restored ruins of **Jerpoint Abbey**, an ancient Cistercian monastery. Founded in the middle of the 12th century by the king of Ossory, it had a relatively brief and very troubled history involving several rivalries with neighbouring institutions, government pressures to keep out Irish monks and finally the dissolution of the monasteries during the year 1540.

Parts of the church retain the Romanesque lines, but the square central tower with its stepped battlements was added during the 15th century. Much sculptural work in the half-restored cloister and the church itself is almost intact, and you can see larger than life carvings of knights and saintly figures, which make inspiring monuments not only to those they honour, but also to the many talented sculptors who worked devotedly at this abbey in the Middle Ages. **55**

The South West

COUNTY CORK

Ireland's most southerly and largest county marries gently rolling farmland with rugged, stony peninsulas and visually delightful bays. Here you will find the people are witty and chatty; after all, this is the home of the blarney.

Cork City (population of 127,000) enjoys all the usual facilities – and traffic jams – of an important commercial and industrial centre, but its atmosphere is entirely unique. This is perhaps because of the River Lee, about which the poet Edmund Spenser wrote:

The spreading Lee, that like an island fayre

Encloseth Cork with his divided flood ...

The dark green waterway which attracts hungry seagulls, elegant white swans and giant freighters to the centre of town accounts for a good deal of the atmospheric mood. So do the steep hills enclosing the urban valleys and the many historic landmarks to be found in the area, of which Corkonians are proud and sentimental.

Incidentally, just to dispel some myths: the name of the city has nothing to do with trees or bottle-stoppers. Cork, an anglicization of *Corcaigh*, is unpromisingly translated as Marshy Place, which is how the area looked back in the 6th century when St Finbarr arrived to found a church and school. In the year 820 the Vikings raided marshy Cork, destroying the institutions and houses, but they liked the lie of the land and so returned to build their own town on the same site. This destruction and rebuilding was repeated like a pattern in the 17th century and then again during the 'Troubles' of 1919-21.

Seeing any city on foot is an opportunity to take a closer look at its monuments and people. You can follow a signposted walking tour, marked with green-and-white 'Tourist Trail' symbols, which takes in the most important sights. This walk starts conveniently at the tourist office itself, which is

ork is the Venice of Ireland, with its city centre built on an island between the two channels of the River Lee.

situated in the Grand Parade, where they sell the booklet explaining the numbered trail. Some highlights are:

Red Abbey, the last remaining vestige of the medieval monasteries in Cork. It is said that in 1690 the Duke of Marlborough witnessed the siege of the city from its tower, his artillery being fired at the town walls from the garden down below.

Patrick Street. The wide main street of Cork is curved because it was built above a river channel. It offers great window-shopping and people promenading; throngs appear on Saturday afternoons.

Make time to visit an Irish whiskey distillery, such as Jameson Distillery at Midleton, and discover the secrets of an age-old tradition.

St Finbarre's Cathedral (Church of Ireland). The latest version, 19th century, follows the lofty French-Gothic style, with arches upon arches; some staid modern statues.

Shandon Church. This is a pepper-pot belfry, which has always been a favourite city landmark. Visitors can climb up through the clockwork intricacies and even play a tune on the bells.

Cork City Gaol, **Sunday's Well**. The cells of the prison have been fully restored to the 19th/early 20th-century style, and even have realistic figures and sound effects.

All over Cork City, many **quaysides** give a fascinating view of the river, bridges and boats, the city skyline and the hills beyond.

Cork is a good centre for excursions. Five miles (8km) to the north, **Blarney Castle** became world famous when Queen Elizabeth I made it a common noun. The owner of the castle, Cormac MacCarthy by family name, and Baron of Blarney, incurred the queen's displeasure by his constant de-

laying tactics and soothing but evasive chatter. 'It's the usual blarney,' the queen is said to have said with despair. Today, tourists climb up to the battlement, lie flat on their backs, hang on to two iron bars and extend the head down backwards to kiss the awkwardly placed stone. This may not assure you gain the 'gift of the gab', but it could cure your fear of heights.

The castle itself, legends aside, is worth a visit, even if mighty hordes of tourists do besiege it every summer. The formidable, square keep was built in the middle of the 15th century, while the private park, in which the castle stands, includes a cool, slightly mysterious dell with ancient occult connections.

In ports around the world, ships are seen with *Cobh* on the stern. You may have asked where it is and how to say it. **Cobh**, Ireland's biggest south coast seaport, is situated about 15 miles (24km) east of Cork City, and pronounced 'Cove', which is also exactly what it means in Irish.

59

From 1849, when Queen Victoria came to visit, until 1922, Cobh was called Queenstown. The port is touched by waves of nostalgia – from the days of the great transatlantic liners and the earlier, more tragic traffic of desperate emigrants fleeing the Irish famine for Canada or America. The Cunard shipping office is now a bank. High above the harbour, the elongated spire of the **Cathedral of St Colman** reaches heavenward. Recitals are given in the summer on the cathedral's 47-bell carillon.

If you're in Midleton, visit the Jameson Heritage Centre in an old, converted whiskey distillery which dates back to the late 18th century. It tells the story of Irish whiskey via an audio-visual presentation, and offers a trail through the distillery and tastings.

The town of **Youghal** (in English pronounced 'Yawl') is a resort with 5 miles (8km) of beach and a long seafaring history. It is renowned for its fine lace, *point d'Irlande*. The town walls from the Middle Ages can still be seen.

On the site of the main town gate is the **clock tower** from 1776. The main street runs right through it with the structure's four narrow floors and belfry rising above an arched platform over the street. The tower is an attractive landmark – except for its past. It was once the prison, and insurrectionists were hanged from the windows to set an example to the populace.

The most impressive monument, **St Mary's Collegiate Church** (Church of Ireland), is thought to have been founded in the 5th century. Most of the present structure went up in the 13th century, with detailed restoration in the 19th. Among the monuments and tombs in the church is one built, in his own honour, by Richard Boyle a wheeler-dealer of the Elizabethan age, the first Earl of Cork. Myrtle Grove, a superb 16th-century house near the churchyard entrance, was the home of Sir Walter Raleigh, once the mayor of Youghal.

Steep green hills on all sides shelter the seaport of **Kinsale**, about 18 miles (29km) south of Cork. As its big harbour is virtually landlocked, it is a joy to sailors and sightseers alike. For a community of less than 2,000 people, Kinsale has unexpected beauty and historical interest. It is also renowned for its restaurants, among the best in south west Ireland.

This was the scene of the famous siege of 1601 in which the Spanish troops, who sailed to the aid of the Irish against Queen Elizabeth, took over the town, but finally suffered a bitter defeat. It set the stage for the 'flight of the Earls', the exodus of the Irish nobility to Europe and the redistribution of their lands. Kinsale became a British naval base.

Nowadays the grandeur of the picturesque **harbour** is put to more productive use by fishing boats, sailing dinghies and yachts. Ashore, there are **fortifications** to explore, the Norman church of St Multose, a small castle where prisoners-of-war were held, and a museum containing the first town charter of Edward III.

Large colonies of breeding and migratory birds inhabit the **Old Head** of Kinsale, 10 miles (16km) beyond the town. A modern lighthouse here is the successor to a beacon dating back to pre-Christian times. It was off the Old Head that a German submarine torpedoed the by now world-famous liner *Lusitania* on 7 May 1915, with the loss of 1,500 lives.

Youghal lighthouse is an important part of the town's long seafaring past.

*B*antry Bay is famous in Irish song and story, and is situated in one of Ireland's most beautiful regions.

The inquest into the horrendous disaster was held in the Kinsale Court House.

On the route from Kinsale to Bantry, there is Clonakilty's model village (to be completed by 1995). It will depict the six main towns of West Cork in model form, complete with a working model of the defunct West Cork Railway.

In West Cork, the town of **Bantry** nestles between steep green hills and a bay that looks like a lake. Whiddy Island, at the head of the bay, was an oil storage depot – until a tanker accident some years ago. The tankers used to enjoy the same advantages which lured the invasion forces here in the 17th and 18th centuries.

The main sight in Bantry itself is Bantry House, a part-Georgian and Victorian stately home set in tropical gardens. The tapestries, paintings and furnishing can be viewed on weekdays from April to mid-October, and the house also offers an Armada Centre, in which an ill-fated attempt by the French to land in Bantry Bay in 1796 is recreated.

Heading counter-clockwise around the bay from Bantry, the highway weaves through progressively more rocky hills until it descends upon **Glengarriff**, where the beauty of the setting and the Mediterranean climate account for its all-year-round popularity.

Ferryboats will take you round the bay from Glengarriff to **Garinish Island**, a 37-acre (15ha) Eden now run by the National Parks and Monument Service. The flora comes from a total of five continents, and the centrepiece of all the horticultural achievement is a stunning walled **Italian garden**, surrounding a pool, with the gentle air of a divine and paradisical perfume factory.

In the 19th century, Garinish was a bleak military outpost. You can climb to the top of the Martello tower, where sentries once kept a lookout for Napoleonic invasion fleets, and survey the luxuriant hills around the bay.

COUNTY KERRY

By any standard this is a spectacular part of the world: the Atlantic in all its moods, lakes designed for lovers or poets, and steep, evergreen mountains. The people, who live in this, the Kingdom of Kerry, are special too – gregarious, outgoing and most generous, perhaps also captured by the spell of their land.

Killarney, the centre of the lakes district, can provide anything a visitor may need, from housing and food to fishing tackle. Seeing the sights here can be accomplished in many ways – by car, coach, bicycle, boat or even by 'jaunting car', a horse-drawn rig driven by a *jarvey* (guide) who knows the territory and how to tell a story on the way.

63

Near Killarney

Due to the difficult terrain and logistical problems, it is best to visit the **Gap of Dunloe** and **Lakes of Killarney** on a fully-organized excursion, usually an all-day trip. The gap, a wild gorge 4 miles (6km) long, can be traversed by pony-back, in a pony trap or, if you insist, on foot. Sound-effects underline the weirdness of the eerie rock-strewn scenery as echoes bounce off the mountains – **MacGillycuddy's Reeks** in the west (the highest range in Ireland), and to the east, **Purple Mountain**. The long trek leads to the shore of the Upper Lake, where the tour continues by boat. The scenery around the lakes – thick forests, stark crags and enchanted islands – could not be more romantic, but there's adventure, too: the **rapids** at Old Weir Bridge.

Muckross Abbey is a friary dating from the 15th century with a massive square tower, a cloister with Gothic arches on two sides, Norman or Romanesque on the others, and an old, weathered yew tree.

Muckross House, nowadays a museum of Kerry crafts and folklore, is surrounded by outstanding gardens. It is also a traditional farm, with old-style buildings and varied animals, including Kerry cows, native to the county.

The 14th-century ruins of **Ross Castle** are set near old copper mines on a peninsula of the Lower Lake. The castle's garrison surrendered to Oliver Cromwell in 1652, awed by the superstition that strange ships spelled doom. The attackers knew the legend and took advantage by bringing armed vessels from Kinsale.

The **Ring of Kerry** may well be the most sensational 112 miles (180km) you have ever driven. Set aside a whole day for the circuit so you have enough time to linger over the sublime sights. The ring is a circular route through hills as steep and round as volcanoes on the way to a coast of rugged cliffs and the most enthralling seascapes.

This round-trip can be made in either direction, but here we proceed clockwise.

A Selection of Hotels and Restaurants in Ireland

Recommended Hotels

Ireland has a huge selection of accommodations. Every location offers budget accommodations, and bed and breakfast can cost as little as £10 per night. For £25 a night, hotels can be luxurious, with en suite bathroom and TV. Those registered with *Bord Fáilte*, the Irish Tourist Board, have guaranteed standards. Some hotels, like Ashford Castle, Dromoland Castle and Waterford Castle offer luxury at £100 per night.

Self-catering accommodation has developed and is often easily rented, although it may be more difficult in peak months.

The international star system awards top hotels 5 stars and 1 star to modest hotels. Guesthouses get 1 to 4 stars.

Local tourist information offices have details of offers in their area. Hotel prices are subject to 12½ percent VAT.

Price categories:

▯▯▯	over £50 per person per night
▯▯	£20 to £50 per person per night
▯	under £20 per person per night

DUBLIN

Ariel House ▯▯

52 Lansdowne Road, Dublin 4
Tel. (01) 668 5512
Fax (01) 668 5845
A guesthouse with a difference, offering well-appointed rooms and a fine Irish welcome. Real comfort at a good price.

Avalon House ▯

55 Aungier Street, Dublin 2
Tel. (01) 475 0001
Fax (01) 475 0303
Budget accommodation with the basic necessitites.

Berkeley Court ▯▯▯

Lansdowne Road, Dublin 4
Tel. (01) 660 1711
Fax (01) 661 7238
Luxurious surroundings have been created in this hotel catering for the discerning guest. Two equally luxurious restaurants.

Clarence Hotel ▯▯

6-8 Wellington Quay, Dublin 2
Tel. (01) 677 6178
Fax (01) 677 7487
Old hotel, by the River Liffey and owned by the famous pop group U2, who have put in some exciting refurbishments.

Conrad   IIII
Earlsfort Terrace, Dublin 2
Tel. (01) 676 5555
Fax (01) 676 5076
Luxury in the Hilton tradition.

Davenport   IIII
Lower Merrion Street, Dublin 2
Tel. (01) 661 6800
Fax (01) 676 6634
Former Plymouth Brethren church relaunched as a luxury hotel with an unusual lobby.

Dublin International   I
Youth Hostel
61 Mountjoy Street, Dublin 7
Tel. (01) 830 1766
Fax (01) 830 1600
Budget-priced accommodation.

Fitzpatrick's   IIII
Killiney Castle
Killiney, Co. Dublin
Tel. (01) 284 0700
Fax (01) 285 0207
Worth the 10-mile (16km) drive from the town centre for its pleasant, spacious rooms.

Isaac Tourist Hostel   I
2 Frenchman's Lane (near bus station), Dublin 2
Tel. (01) 874 9321
Fax (01) 874 1574
Dormitory accommodation near the city centre.

Jury's Christchurch Inn   II
Christchurch Place, Dublin 8
Tel. (01) 475 0111
Fax (01) 475 0488
New economy-class hotel near the city centre. Adequately if sparsely fitted.

Kilronan House   II
70 Adelaide Road, Dublin 2
Tel. (01) 475 5266
Fax (01) 878 2841
Long-established guesthouse.

Kingswood   II
Country House
Kingswood, Naas Road, Dublin 22
Tel. (01) 459 2428
Fax (01) 459 2207
Unlikely setting off the main road from Dublin to the south and west, comfortable and welcoming.

Mount Herbert   II
Herbert Road, Dublin 4
Tel. (01) 668 4321
Fax (01) 660 7077
Economy-class popular hotel with its own restaurant.

Shelbourne   IIII
St Stephen's Green, Dublin 2
Tel. (01) 676 6471
Fax (01) 661 6006
Dublin's oldest hotel (150 years) retaining plenty of character.

Stauntons on the Green ▌▌
83 St Stephen's Green, Dublin 2
Tel. (01) 478 2300
Georgian guesthouse with a very friendly welcome.

Stephen's Hall ▌▌
14-17 Lower Leeson Street, Dublin 2
Tel. (01) 661 0585
Fax (01) 661 0606
Luxurious, but reasonably priced, self-catering accommodation.

The Towers ▌▌▌
Ballsbridge, Dublin 4
Tel. (01) 660 5000
Fax (01) 660 5540
Last word in luxury: sumptuous rooms well worth the prices.

Tinakilly Country ▌▌▌ House Hotel & Restaurant
Rathnew, Co. Wicklow
Tel. (0404) 69274
Fax (0404) 67806
Elegant mansion in setting near the sea, 30 miles from Dublin.

Trident Holiday Homes ▌▌
2 Sandymount Village Centre, Dublin 4
Tel. (01) 668 3534
Fax (01) 660 6465
Holiday homes and apartments to rent in various counties.

CORK

Blue Haven ▌▌
Kinsale
Tel. (021) 772209
Fax (021) 774268
Individually-styled rooms, and a fine restaurant.

Cork International ▌ Hostel
1 Redclyffe, Western Road, Cork
Tel. (021) 543289
Fax (021) 343715
Inexpensive youth hostel.

Fitzpatrick's ▌▌▌ Silver Springs
Tivoli, Cork
Tel. (021) 507533
Fax (021) 507641
Luxury hotel on eastern road to Cork City – excellent facilities.

Forte Travelodge ▌▌
Kinsale Road, Cork
Tel. (021) 310722
Fax (021) 310707
Well-run, modestly priced modern family hotel.

Jury's ▌▌▌
Western Road, Cork
Tel. (021) 276622
Fax (021) 274477
Luxury-class accommodation and restaurants on west side of Cork.

Morrisons Island   III
Morrisons Quay, Cork
Tel. (021) 275858
Fax (021) 275833
Luxurious self-catering, en-suite facilities, also has a restaurant.

Westlodge Hotel   II
Bantry, Co. Cork
Tel. (027) 50360
Fax (027) 50438
Modern hotel with all amenities.

Great Southern   III
Eyre Square, Galway
Tel. (091) 64041
Fax (091) 66704
19th-century railway hotel, which has been recently refurbished.

KERRY

Benner's   II
Main Street, Dingle
Tel. (066) 51638
Fax (066) 51412
Comfortable hotel situated in the town centre, with all amenities.

Crutch's Country House   II
Fermoyle Beach, Castlegregory
Tel. (066) 38118
Fax (066) 38159
Cosy, rural atmosphere, offering all home comforts, based in a idyllic location near an inviting and lengthy sandy beach.

Doyle's   II
John Street, Dingle
Tel. (066) 51174
Fax (066) 51816
Has a famous seafood restaurant – lively and full of character.

Sheen Falls Lodge   III
Kenmare
Tel. (064) 41600
Fax (064) 41386
Magnificent hotel in a setting to match, with good facilities.

The Towers   II
Glenbeigh
Tel. (066) 68212
Fax (066) 68260
Old and comfortably refurbished, with restaurant.

KILKENNY

Castletroy Park   III
Dublin Road, Limerick
Tel. (061) 335566
Fax (061) 331117
Ultra-modern hotel, all facilities.

Club House   II
Patrick Street, Kilkenny
Tel. (056) 21994
Fax (056) 21994
Historic 18th-century hotel, well refurbished; its many mementoes include a set of witty 19th-century political cartoons.

69

Foulksrath Castle Hostel
Jenkinstown, Co. Kilkenny
Tel. (056) 67674
Budget-priced youth hostel.

Hotel Kilkenny
College Road, Kilkenny
Tel. (056) 62000
Fax (056) 65984
Pleasant and modern hotel with all amenities, including a health and leisure centre.

Lacken House
Dublin Road, Kilkenny
Tel. (056) 61085
Fax (056) 62435
Good guesthouse accommodation, with widely-acclaimed restaurant.

LIMERICK and SHANNON

Ballyteigue House
Bruree, Co. Limerick
Tel. (063) 90575
18th-century Georgian farmhouse, all rooms en suite.

Carrygerry House
near Shannon Airport
Tel. (061) 472339
Fax (061) 472123
This 18th-century house has been converted to a hotel with rooms set around a courtyard, and a fine conservatory restaurant.

Dromoland Castle
Newmarket-on-Fergus
Tel. (061) 368144
Fax (061) 363355
19th-century baronial pile, now a luxury hotel in fine grounds.

Limerick International Hostel
1 Pery Square, Limerick
Tel. (061) 314672
Fax (061) 312107
Youth hostel accommodation.

MAYO

Ashford Castle
Cong, Co. Mayo
Tel. (092) 46003
Fax (092) 46260
Former 19th-century mansion of the Guinness family, the last word in luxury holiday accommodation.

Olde Railway Hotel
The Mall, Westport, Co. Mayo
Tel. (098) 25166
Fax (098) 25090
Very agreeable riverside hotel, full of artefacts and bonhomie; pub and restaurant serving food.

Quiet Man Hostel
Abbey Street, Cong, Co. Mayo
Tel. (092) 46089
Fax (092) 46448
Budget accommodation.

WATERFORD

Granville ||
The Quay, Waterford
Tel. (051) 55111
Fax (051) 70307
Historic, comfortable hotel by the River Suir.

Lismore Hostel |
Glengarra, Lismore,
Co. Waterford
Tel. (058) 54390
Youth hostel accommodation.

Prendiville's ||
Cork Road, Waterford
Tel. (051) 78851
Bedrooms are all en suite. Locals dine in the restaurant.

The Tower ||
The Mall, Waterford
Tel. (051) 75801
Fax (051) 70129
Luxury hotel in the city centre, the many amenities include an indoor swimming pool.

Waterford Castle ||||
The Island, Ballinakilly,
Waterford
Tel. (051) 78203
Fax (051) 79316
Historic castle, now an impressive luxury hotel, with comprehensive facilities including a golf course.

WEXFORD

Marlfield House ||||
Gorey, Co. Wexford
Tel. (055) 21124
Fax (055) 21572
Stylish country mansion recently converted into an exquisite hotel offering accommodation to a high standard, with gourmet restaurant.

Rosslare Harbour Hotel |
Goulding Street, Rosslare
Tel. (053) 33399
Fax (053) 33624
Budget-class hotel rooms in this hotel, based at the major seaport.

Sir Richard and ||
Lady Levinge
Clomahon House, Bunclody,
Co. Wexford
Tel. (054) 77253
Fax (054) 77956
Classy, country-house living, with rooms furnished in the grandest manner, and cuisine of a matching high standard.

White's Hotel ||
Wexford
Tel. (053) 22311
Fax (053) 45000
Old hotel brought up-to-date by renovation in more recent times. Full facilities and some historic mementos.

71

NORTHERN IRELAND

Belfast
International Hostel
11 Saintfield Road, Belfast
BT8 4AE
Tel. (0232) 647865
Fax (0232) 247439
Youth hostel accommodation in a fairly central location.

Chestnut Inn
28 Lower Square,
Castewellan, Co. Down
Tel. (03967 78247
A well-established, 100-year old family-run inn set in an attractive country town.

Bushmills Inn
25 Main Street,
Bushmills, Co. Antrim
Tel. (02657) 32339
Fax (02657) 32048
An old coaching inn converted into a comfortable hotel with its own historic character, and high quality accommodation.

Culloden
142 Bangor Road,
Holywood, Co. Down
Tel. (0232) 425223
Fax (0232) 426777
Northern Ireland's most luxurious hotel, based on the shores of the Belfast Lough.

Londonderry Arms
20 Harbour Road,
Carnlough, Co. Antrim
Tel. (0574) 885255
Fax (0574) 885263
Historic hotel, situated in coastal setting in scenic Glens of Antrim.

Moohan's Fiddlestone
15 Main Street, Belleek,
Co. Fermanagh
Tel. (036565) 8008
Traditional Irish guesthouse and pub in renowned pottery village.

Plaza
15 Brunswick Street, Belfast
BT2 7GE
Tel. (0232) 333555
Fax (0232) 232999
Lxurious hotel near to the city's 'Golden Mile' of nightclubs.

Rathlin Guesthouse
Rathlin Island, Co. Antrim
Tel. (02657) 63917
The most isolated spot in Northern Ireland, the only accommodation on Rathlin Island.

Tyrella House
Clanmaghery Road,
Downpatrick, Co. Down
Tel. (0396) 85422
18th-century country house, with Georgian restaurant, own grounds, and beach.

Recommended Restaurants

The choice of restaurants in Ireland has increased enormously over the last few years, with establishments offering Chinese, Indian, Japanese, Malaysian and Thai cuisine opening up in many areas. A few restaurants serve authentic Irish food, like cabbage and bacon or Dublin coddle (bacon, kidney, sausage and onion), but often hotels and guesthouses serve excellent, home-made food.

While Cork, including Kinsale, is acknowledged as one of the best areas for eating out, Belfast has developed hugely, and prices compete with those in the Republic. Some restaurants have a full licence to serve any drinks; otherwise, they serve wine only and not beer. Special tourist menus available are a cheaper alternative for lunch and dinner.

The VAT rate on restaurant meals is 12½ percent. In addition, some restaurants may add a 12½ percent service charge. To give you an idea of prices, we have used the following symbols for a three-course meal for one excluding wine:

| | £10 or more |
| | Under £10 |

DUBLIN

Abbey Tavern
Howth, Dublin
Tel. (01) 839 0307
16th-century inn serving seafood and offering Irish entertainment.

Bad Ass Café
9-11 Crown Alley,
Dublin 2
Tel. (01) 671 2596
A big favourite: pizzas, steaks and burgers, lively atmosphere.

Bewleys
12 Westmoreland Street,
Dublin 2
Tel. (01) 677 6761
78 Grafton Street, Dublin 2
Tel. (01) 677 6761
Historic venues, always packed.

Bon Appetit
9 James Terrace, Malahide,
Co. Dublin
Tel. (01) 845 0314
Fine gourmet cuisine, specialising in game, poultry and seafood.

73

Commons

Newman House, 85-86
St Stephen's Green, Dublin 2
Tel. (01) 475 2597
One of Dublin's classiest and most elegant restaurants, contemporary decor and classical menus.

Conrad Hotel

Earlsfort Terrace, Dublin 2
Tel. (01) 676 5555
The Alexandra Restaurant serves classy gourmet cuisine, while the Plurabelle Restaurant is informal, and offers simpler menus.

Cooke's Café

14 South William Street, Dublin 2
Tel. (01) 679 0536
One of Dublin's 'in' places, and so guaranteed to have an energetic and conversational buzz.

Dillond

21 Suffolk Street, Dublin 2
Tel. (01) 677 4804
Cosy, intimate restaurant in the city centre, specializing in steaks and fish, with some Irish dishes.

Dobbin's Wine Bistro

15 Stephen's Lane, Dublin 2
Tel. (01) 676 4679
Long-established restaurant serving fresh produce and offering a lengthy wine list – very popular for lunch and dinner.

Ernies

Mulberry Gardens,
Donnybrook, Dublin 4
Tel. (01) 269 3300
Classical restaurant built around a mulberry tree, decorated with over 100 Irish paintings, and specializing in game and seafood.

Footplate Brasserie

Kingsbridge Station, Dublin 8
Tel. (01) 703 2100
Railway stations are not always associated with the most pleasant surroundings and tasty food, but this relatively new place means business and is excellent.

Gallagher's Boxty House

20-21 Temple Bar, Dublin 2
Tel. (01) 677 2762
One of the few restaurants in the country specialising in traditional and authentic Irish cuisine has a decor to match, rustic interiors and several open fireplaces.

Kingswood Country House

Kingswood, Naas Road,
Dublin 22
Tel. (01) 459 2428
An authentic country house with a restaurant serving home cooking in a rural setting, despite the proximity of the motorway.

Le Coq Hardi

35 Pembroke Road,
Ballsbridge, Dublin 4
Tel. (01) 668 4130
Expensive French restaurant, said
to have the largest wine cellar in
the whole of Ireland.

Mitchell's Cellars

21 Kildare Street, Dublin 2
Tel. (01) 668 0367
Bistro-style dishes served in what
were once the cellars of the wine
shop above. Extensive wine list.

Oisin's Irish Restaurant

31 Upper Camden Street,
Dublin 2
Tel. (01) 475 3433
Quite expensive, but offering the
rarity of traditional Irish dishes
made with local produce.

Old Dublin

91 Francis Street, Dublin 8
Tel. (01) 454 2028
Atmospheric restaurant in the old
part of Dublin, serves Russian and
Scandinavian food.

Patrick Guilbaud

46 James Place, Dublin 2
Tel. (01) 676 4192
Dublin's best known and probably
most expensive restaurant, creat-
ing classy, original French dishes
from the freshest Irish ingredients.

Red Bank

7 Church Street, Skerries,
Co. Dublin
Tel. (01) 849 1005
Family-run seafood restaurant of
great character, in fishing village.

Restaurant na Mara

Dun Laoghaire, Co. Dublin
Tel. (01) 280 0509
More good eats, this time in part
of Ireland's oldest railway station
which has been converted into a
classical restaurant specializing in
gourmet fish dishes.

Riverbank

10 Burgh Quay, Dublin 2
Tel. (01) 677 0182
Agreeable restaurant looking out
over River Liffey, serving meals
all day.

Roches Bistro

12 New Street, Malahide,
Co. Dublin
Tel. (01) 845 2777
Cosy restaurant serving seafood
dishes in a mainly French cuisine.

101 Talbot

101-102 Talbot Street (first floor),
Dublin 1
Tel. (01) 874 5011
Bright, cheerful restaurant serving
inexpensive and typically popular
Mediterranean dishes.

75

Wong's
Clontarf Road, Dublin 3
Tel. (01) 833 4400
Exquisitely-styled Chinese restaurant with cuisine to match.

Winding Stair Café
40 Lower Ormond Quay, Dublin 1
Tel. (01) 873 3292
Inexpensive café in bookshop.

CORK

Ballymaloe House
Shanagarry, Co. Cork
Tel. (021) 652531
On a farm, the restaurant is run by the Allen family, noted worldwide for their gourmet writing.

Blue Haven
Pearse Street, Kinsale, Co. Cork
Tel. (021) 772209
The garden room restaurant serves seafood and vegetarian dishes.

Clifford's
18 Dyke Parade, Cork
Tel. (021) 275333
Gourmet cookery, traditional Irish and French dishes.

Forte Travelodge
Kinsale Road, Cork
Tel. (021) 310722
Reasonably priced all-day food in bright, clean surroundings.

Mary Ann's Bar and Contented Sole Restaurant
Castletownshend, Co. Cork
Tel. (028) 36146
Seafood restaurant with cheaper menus served from the bar; the restaurant is set in a small, idyllic seaside village in West Cork.

McDonald's
4-5 Winthrop Street, Cork
Tel. (021) 272175
Douglas Shopping Centre,
Douglas, Cork
Tel. (021) 364456
Hamburgers, milk shakes, and all the fast food 'old favourites'.

Presidents' Restaurant
Longueville House,
near Mallow, Co. Cork
Tel. (022) 47156
An upmarket 18th-century mansion is the setting for this restaurant with walls lined with portraits of Ireland's presidents. Has its own vineyard, which produces a wine similar to a Riesling.

Shiro Japanese Dinner House
Ahakista, Durrus, Co. Cork
Tel. (027) 67030
Authentic and expensive Japanese cuisine, but since the restaurant is small and very popular, advance booking is essential.

GALWAY

Brannigans ▐▐

36 Upper Abbeygate Street,
Galway
Tel. (091) 65974
Boasting an exotic Victorian-style interior; Brannigans features both Cajun and Mexican cuisine.

Currach Restaurant ▐▐

Corrib Great Southern Hotel,
Dublin Road, Galway
Tel. (091) 55281
New restaurant with fine views.

Galleon ▐

Salthill, Galway
Tel. (091) 22963
Long background, and well-priced menu: fish, steaks and Irish stew, served in a seaside setting.

GBC Restaurant ▐
and Coffee Shop

Williamsgate Street, Galway
Tel. (091) 63087
Inexpensive and centrally located, using as much fresh local produce as possible.

Oyster Room ▐▐

Great Southern Hotel,
Eyre Square, Galway
Tel. (091) 64041
Noted restaurant in centre of the city, serving first-class cuisine.

KERRY

Beginish ▐▐

Green Street, Dingle
Tel. (066) 51588
Elegant seafood restaurant, with a warm welcome from the owner and staff.

Doyle's Seafood Bar ▐▐

John Street, Dingle
Tel. (066) 51174
One of the country's best-known restaurants. It's cramped, but it's also full of life and character – a fun place to eat.

Old School House ▐▐

Knockeens, Cahirciveen
Tel. (066) 72426
Family-run seafood restaurant in a converted schoolhouse. Staff are very friendly, and dishes are made with fresh home-grown produce.

Park Hotel ▐▐

Kenmare
Tel. (064) 41200
First-class cuisine in an elegant 5-star hotel.

Pizza Time ▐

Innisfallen Shopping Centre,
Killarney
Tel. (064) 35380
Friendly restaurant, with a warm atmosphere and fully-licensed bar. **77**

Sheen Falls Lodge Hotel

Kenmare
Tel. (064) 41600
Imaginative and colourful menus using fresh local produce, served in a restaurant overlooking the most spectacular waterfalls.

The Laurels

Main Street, Killarney
Tel. (064) 31149
A long-established and family-run restaurant serving very good food. The menu also includes vegetarian and gluten-free dishes.

LIMERICK and SHANNON

Copper Room

Jury's Hotel,
Ennis Road, Limerick
Tel. (061) 327777
Classical French cuisine is served in this intimate restaurant located in a top-rated hotel.

Doolin Café

Doolin, Co. Clare
Tel. (065) 74429
A friendly, informal atmosphere is the hallmark of the Doolin café in its seaside village location. It offers wholesome food, and good music as well as a range of books to browse through.

Dromoland Castle

Newmarket-on-Fergus, Co. Clare
Tel. (061) 368144
The dining room in Dromoland Castle is spectacular, with superb, elaborate table settings and grand-chandeliers overhead to complete the scene, an excellent backdrop for the gourmet cuisine.

Lindbergh Carvery and Buffet

Shannon Airport
Tel. (061) 61444
Spacious restaurant with friendly staff, and serving a good selection of traditional Irish dishes, including famous Limerick ham.

MacCloskey's

Bunratty House Mews,
Bunratty, Co. Clare
Tel. (061) 364082
This is an exquisite gourmet cellar restaurant, serving classic cuisine. Always bustling, it has plenty of clientèle to create an ambience for a memorable evening.

Manuel's Seafood Restaurant

Kilkee, Co. Clare
Tel. (065) 56211
Modern restaurant, with brightly decorated interior, specializing in seafood and shellfish, and lovely vegetarian dishes.

Mustard Seed

Adare, Co. Limerick
Tel. (061) 396451
Thatched roof restaurant with an original Irish kitchen, featuring creative cooking by the owner.

WATERFORD

Dwyers

8 Mary Street, Waterford
Tel. (051) 77478
A small gourmet restaurant with a short, but nevertheless original menu.

Grand Hotel

Tramore
Tel. (051) 81414
Excellent hotel with a very lively restaurant.

Ship Restaurant

Dunmore East
Tel. (051) 83141
Fresh seafood served in informal surroundings.

WEXFORD

Cellar Restaurant

Horetown House, Fouksmills, Co. Wexford
Tel. (051) 63771
A 300-year-old cellar, complete with blazing log fire, specializing in country house cuisine.

Country Kitchen

White's Hotel,
George Street, Wexford
Tel. (053) 22311
Delicious country farmhouse-style food, served all day.

Marlfield House

Gorey, Co. Wexford
Tel. (055) 21124
An interesting mixture of French and Irish cuisine on the menu, which includes a selection of fish dishes. A classic, country house setting for a romantic evening out.

WICKLOW

Grand Hotel

Wicklow Town
Tel. (0404) 67337
Comfortable restaurant with very friendly staff serving bar food all day over the counter.

Hunter's

Rathnew
Tel. (0404) 40106
An historic 18th-century coaching inn with fine gardens; restaurant specializes in exquisite and tasty cooking.

Old Rectory

Wicklow Town
Tel. (0404) 67048
Fine gourmet cooking.

79

Pizza del Forno

Wicklow Town
Tel. (0404) 67075
Excellent family restaurant, with red checked table-cloths. Serves pizzas, steaks and vegetarian food.

Roundwood Inn

Roundwood
Tel. (01) 281 8107
Gourmet menus influenced by the German cuisine, also good bar food, featuring goulash, Irish stew, smoked salmon.

NORTHERN IRELAND

Bananas

4 Clarence Street,
Belfast BT2 8DX
Tel. (0232) 339999
Friendly restaurant situated in the centre of Belfast, and serving such specialities as lamb kebab.

Elbow

45 Dublin Road, Belfast BT2 7HD
Tel. (0232) 233003
Well-rated bar restaurant serving scampi and steak.

La Belle Epoque

103 Great Victoria Street,
Belfast BT2 7AG
Tel. (0232) 323244
French gourmet restaurant, which serves game in season.

Linen Hall Library

17 Donegall Square North,
Belfast BT1 5GB
Tel. (0232) 321707
Café in reading room.

Portaferry Hotel

10 The Strand, Portaferry,
Co. Down
Tel. (02477) 28231
Quayside spot for fresh seafood, including stuffed mussels, fried oysters and turbot. Also bar food.

Roscoff

Lesley House, Shaftesbury
Square, Belfast BT2 7DB
Tel. (0232) 331532
The city's most famous gourmet restaurant, in the French tradition, serving such delights as crispy duck confit and tasty roast sikka venison.

Saints & Scholars

3 University Street, Belfast
BT7 1FY
Tel. (0232) 325137
Lively spot set in the university quarter, with specialities like deep fried brie and cassoulet.

Slieve Donard Hotel

Newcastle, Co. Down
Tel. (03967) 23681
The Dog's Head Grill Bar is a very welcoming and popular venue.

Leaving Killarney, the road goes past lush lakeland. The first town on the route, **Kenmare**, is famous for lacemaking and the fish which fill its estuary. North of the small resort of Castlecove, a couple of miles off the main road, are the ruins of **Staigue Fort**.

A 2,500-year-old stronghold, one of Ireland's main archaeological wonders – this is an almost circular structure about 90ft (27m) across with a wall measuring 18ft (5m). It predates the invention of cement, so its building and survival was quite a feat.

Near Caherdaniel, the home of Daniel O'Connell ('the Liberator'), has been fully restored and is now a museum. Game fishing is one of the lures for visitors to Waterville, as well as the scenery nearby: pitiless granite mountains on one side of the road, green fields and the sea on the other.

A bridge connects **Valentia Island**, with its high cliffs and vegetation, to the mainland at Portmagee. The island was the European terminus of the first Atlantic cable (1866), making possible the first telegraphic contact with America.

Shamrock Curtain

Travelling in the west of Ireland you may suddenly cross the Shamrock Curtain, an invisible cultural frontier. The signs are printed in hard-to-decipher Gaelic letters and the people talk in a cryptic ancient tongue. This means you've stumbled into the **Gaeltacht**, pockets of green scattered over seven counties. They make up the main line of resistance to the predominance of that mighty international language, English. The Dublin government actively supports the Gaeltacht efforts to keep the old language and culture alive.

Courses in Irish are offered in the Gaeltacht every summer. If you can't attend any, don't be afraid to go into the area – it's quite rare to find anyone who can't also speak English.

Off Valentia, the Skelligs Rocks rise abruptly from the ocean, shrouded with mystery and birds – 20,000 pairs of gannets alone. Take a trip to the Skelligs Heritage Centre or tour the islands in a special boat. The crag caves on Castle Island are newly-opened rivals to the Aillwee Cave in the Burren and, also impressive – they are nearly 2 miles (4km) long.

On the north shore of the peninsula, green hills plunge to sea-level and cliffs complete the descent. **Dingle Bay** seems startlingly wide and the Dingle peninsula looks almost like another country.

From Glenbeigh to Killorglin, the head of the bay is almost totally protected from the rough sea by huge sandbars extending from either shore. **Rossbeigh Strand**, with its 4 miles (6km) of golden sand, is a dream beach.

The last town on the ring, **Killorglin**, saves all its energy for three days in August and a mad pagan pageant called the Puck Fair, during which time a mountain goat presides over round-the-clock festivities.

To the north, **Tralee**, with a population of 17,000, the administrative centre of County Kerry, owes its fame to the songwriter William Mulchinock (1820-64). *The Rose of Tralee* and its author are honoured in a monument in the town park. Rose also calls the tune of Tralee's annual festival in September when girls of Irish descent from many countries compete in a beauty contest and the winner is crowned Rose of Tralee.

Kerry the Kingdom offers three experiences all in one. Kerry in Colour is an audio-visual presentation of the splendours of Kerry; the County Museum gives details of Kerry history since 5000 BC; and the Geraldine Experience reconstructs life in medieval Tralee. A steam railway, with a locomotive from the old Tralee-Dingle railway, links the town with the restored, early 19th-century windmill at Blennerville, 1½ miles (2.5km) away.

Apart from these popular attractions, Tralee is the gateway to the Dingle peninsula, a long, dramatic finger which points some 30 miles (48km) into the Atlantic. On the south shore, amidst severe cliffs and rocky coves, a sandbar grows into an arc of beach jutting more than halfway across the bay. **Inch Strand's** 4 miles (6km) of sand slide gently into the sea. Behind the bathers and suntanners, archaeologists potter about the dunes, where inhabitants of prehistoric ages left meaningful debris.

The small fishing port and resort of **Dingle** claims to be the single most westerly town in Europe. From here to land's end all the hamlets are Irish-speaking parts of the Gaeltacht (see p.81), where folklore and traditional language are still thoughtfully preserved.

This is very harsh farming country, where the old stone walls are overrun with shrubs, and hardy vines divide skimpy parcels of land.

*A*s the well-known Irish song will tell you: 'You can view the lakes of Killarney from an Irish jaunting car'.

You'll see the sheep grazing on even the precipitous fields. They usually have splotches of red or blue dye daubed on their backs to affirm ownership and provide a means of telling the different flocks apart.

The western part of the peninsula is very rich territory for archaeologists. In one area, the Fahan group alone consists of a staggering 400 *clochans* (beehive-shaped stone huts), along with forts and other ancient structures.

For a spectacular panorama, drive up the **Connor Pass** (at an altitude of 1,500ft/457m) and see the sea to the north and south, mountains and lakes to the east and west. The near-sighted – or fog-bound – can simply admire the wild fuchsia and heather beside the road.

The West

LIMERICK

By the time the waters of the River Shannon have reached Limerick (pop. 52,000) in the west, they have flowed over 170 miles (274km) through thick and thin: from narrow streams and howling rapids to lakes and efficient locks. After Limerick, an important seaport and industrial centre, they still have another 60 miles (97km) to travel through the Shannon estuary to the open Atlantic.

This major position at the meeting of the river and its tidal waters assured the city a long and often violent history. The Danes were first on the scene. Their belligerent policy provoked repeated attacks by the neighbouring native Irish, who finally drove them out.

The Anglo-Normans in turn captured the place with the unpretentious name of *Luimneach* – in English 'Bare Spot'. King John visited Limerick in 1210 and ordered the construction of a **bridge** and

castle, which still survive and which have been extensively renovated. However, most of the town walls, behind which the townsfolk gathered during times of siege, were pulled down in the 18th century to make way for civic expansion.

The most memorable siege was endured after the Battle of the Boyne (1690), when the Irish supporters of James II (see p.18) retired to Limerick pursued by William of Orange. In spite of heroic efforts, the losers eventually lost again.

The Treaty of Limerick, which allowed the garrison to leave with honour, softened the blow by guaranteeing the Irish people freedom of religion. But this was repudiated by the then English Parliament and so today Limerick carries the title of 'City of the Violated Treaty.'

Limerick's major historical monument, the 800-year-old **St Mary's Cathedral** (Church of Ireland), spans many eras of architecture and art. The great square tower complements the arched Irish-Romanesque west door, while 15th-century carved misericords under the choir seats show free-ranging imagination with representations of an angel, animals such as an eagle, a goat, and a dragon and other figures in relief.

The cathedral grounds form the background for a colourful historical audio-visual show with sound and lights.

St John's Cathedral, (a Catholic cathedral), was constructed in neo-Gothic style, and claims to have the highest spire in Ireland (280ft/85m). Next to the cathedral, reconstruction and restoration work on a grand scale is reviving St John's Square, an elegant 18th-century urban ensemble.

King John's Castle, built in the 13th century, dominates the view of the majestic River Shannon from Sarsfield Bridge.

The River Shannon

Briefly deviating from our general progress around the coast, here's an inland foray down the River Shannon, but if you don't have the inclination to hire a boat, you can also visit the attractions along the Shannon by car or bus.

Most of the cruiser-hiring is at **Carrick-on-Shannon**, the 'capital' of County Leitrim, and boasting the superb Costelloe Chapel of Main Street.

Downstream from Carrick, the river runs into Lough Corry, the first of many interconnected lakes in the Shannon basin. **Lough Ree**, halfway down, is 16 miles (26km) long and 7 miles (11km) wide in places, with deserted wooded islands.

The main cross-country roads ford the Shannon at the central market town of **Athlone** with a medieval castle, overlooking the Shannon Bridge. A museum has been opened inside.

At a bend in the river is **Clonmacnois**, an ancient monastic settlement founded in the 6th C. by St Ciaran, which became a major medieval university. Nearby you can follow a 5½-mile (9km) trip along the Clonmacnois & West Offaly Railway.

Just 4 miles (6km) south of Clonmacnois, a 16-arch bridge marks Shannonbridge, and at Shannon Harbour the Grand Canal from Dublin meets the river. Portumna is a fishing and boating resort with a new marina.

Lough Derg is the largest of the Shannon lakes – 25 miles (40km) long and up to 3 miles (5km) wide with islets and fair green hills beyond – a perfect end to the trip.

This is just as well because dangerous rapids abound below **Killaloe**, a prudent place to abandon ship. Killaloe was once a great ecclesiastical centre, where **St Flannan's Cathedral** (Church of Ireland) has been restored to its 12th-century glory. The richly-carved Romanesque doorway (now blocked) is said to be the entrance to the tomb of King Murtagh O'Brien of Munster (d. 1120). The granite shaft nearby, from about the year 1000, bears a bilingual inscription in Runic and Ogham letters – a foretaste of today's Irish-English road signs.

The 18th-century waterfront Custom House is being fully restored to house the priceless Hunt collection of antiquities and *objets d'art*, currently kept by the University of Limerick.

The word 'limerick' comes from the merry refrain 'Will you come up to Limerick?', part of an old parlour game, in which the participants had to make up a nonsense verse.

Shannon Airport reinforces Limerick's historic role as a centre of commerce. It opened in 1945, making its mark in those adventurous days before fast and non-stop transatlantic travel became the order of the day. Nervous passengers who were waiting for their planes to be refuelled were offered a diversion – the chance to buy luxury goods exempt from tax. Thus the world's first duty-free shop grew into a shopping centre, and the airport became the hub of an industrial development with tax concessions.

The Shannon Free Airport Development Company then took over the management of **Bunratty Castle**, and turned it into a busy tourist attraction.

The castle, a few miles from the airport, has been restored. At night 'Medieval Banquets' are recreated for visitors by professional Irish entertainers in period costumes accompanied by traditional music from the Irish harp.

The latest addition to the Bunratty tourist complex is a **Folk Park** containing replicas of typical old houses of the Shannon region. The peat fires are kept burning, as if the people had just stepped out to milk a cow or catch a fish.

A new marina has been built in **Kilrush**, where the heritage centre details the history of the town and Scattery, a nearby island and Christian settlement. At Foynes, you can visit the flying boat museum which has old newsreels among its many attractions.

The administrative centre of County Clare, **Ennis**, has a 13th-century friary, which in the Middle Ages had 350 friars and an amazing 600 students. The buildings were expanded and revamped over the years, and finally fully renovated in the 1950s.

87

THE BURREN

North west of Ennis, over 200 square miles (518sq km) of County Clare belongs to **the Burren** – a set of geological formations. Glaciers and the erosion of ages have created limestone 'pavements' – horizontal slabs divided by fissures, like the aftermath of an earthquake.

Though it is sometimes described as a moonscape, the Burren is anything but barren; it is a quiet world of small animals, birds, butterflies and Mediterranean flowers. It may seem hostile to human habitation, but the profusion of forts and tombs proves it has supported a population for several centuries.

Geologists, botanists and archaeologists have field trips on the 'pavements', and speleologists enjoy checking out the caves. Over 25 miles (40km) of caves have been fully explored. Most of them are for experts only, but anyone can visit Aillwee Cave, south east of Ballyvaughan (open April **88** to October).

In Kilfenora, a village on the edge of this plain, citizens have established the original **Burren Display Centre**, as a quick and pleasant way to get your Burren bearings.

Kilfenora Cathedral, dating from about the 12th century, is noted for its sculptured monuments, and the village has many high crosses.

The **Cliffs of Moher**, just 6 miles (10km) north west of Lahinch, tower 700ft (213m) over the Atlantic Ocean. From O'Brien's Tower, an outpost near to the edge, the spectacle moves the spirit: the cliff-faces stand above the sea posing for pictures, the horizontal layers are as easily defined with the eye as the storeys of a glass skyscraper. You watch a great wave crash against the foot of the cliff but the thump is heard a little late, like the report of a distant artillery shell. Many thousands of sea birds live on the cliffs.

The town of **Lisdoonvarna** is famous as a spa and has its own atmosphere of romance. The springs produce waters which are rich in numerous

The cliffs of Moher rise dramatically from the Atlantic Ocean offering spectacular views and refreshing walks.

minerals, including sulphur, iron and iodine, thought to be good for rheumatic conditions and as a general tonic.

Though not very romantic in itself, the town has gained a reputation as a match-making mecca and indeed people from all over the country have arrived in Lisdoonvarna in an attempt to find a mate, making Ireland's first spa their last resort. More recently folk music festivals have broadened the appeal, and also lowered the average age at local dances.

Across the border in County Galway, the area around the town of Gort has a number of historic and powerful literary associations.

Lady Gregory, co-founder of the Abbey Theatre, lived in **Coole Park**, now a national forest. The novel 'autograph tree' here is inscribed with the initials of some of her famous visitors – Augustus John, John Masefield, Sean O'Casey and one of the very few who is instantly recognized by his initials: George Bernard Shaw.

Four miles (6km) north east of Gort, William Butler Yeats bought himself a 16th-century tower, **Thoor Ballylee**, and decided to live there – it is as inspiring a place as any poet could pick for a domicile. You can wander around this piece of romantic architecture with its spiral stairwell, alcoves and just outside the window, its very own burbling stream.

The spa town of Lisdoonvarna is famous for its annual match-making festival in September.

GALWAY

The main city of the western province of Connacht, **Galway** (pop. 51,000) is a port, resort, administrative and cultural centre. In medieval times it prospered as a city-state, but withered in the 17th-century after two disasters: prolonged sieges by the forces of Thomas Cromwell and, four decades later, by William of Orange. However, remnants of the old glory still shine in a few corners of the renewed city.

The **Collegiate Church of St Nicholas** (belonging to the Church of Ireland) was begun by the Anglo-Normans in the year 1320. Following the local tradition, Columbus came to pray here before his voyage to America, and the locals like to think he was checking out the 6th-century transatlantic explorer, St Brendan. There is a pyramid-shaped steeple on top of the triple-naved church, full of stonecarvings.

During Galway's heyday 14 families, mostly of Welsh and Norman descent, formed a sort of medieval Mafia controlling the economic and political life of the town. Their common enemy, the O'Flaherty family, inspired the inscription (1549) over the old town gate: 'From the fury of the O'Flaherties, good Lord deliver us.' Of the countless 'tribes' in Galway, the Lynch family left the most memories and monuments.

Lynch's Castle, a townhouse dating from 1600, is decorated with some excellent stonework, gargoyles and carved window-frames. This rare building has now been lovingly restored and houses a bank.

Another reminder of the Lynches is the 'Lynch Memorial Window' with a plaque recounting the macabre story of James Lynch FitzStephen – Mayor of Galway in 1493 – who condemned and executed his own son, Walter, for murder. Judge Lynch had to be the hangman because nobody else would agree to carry out the sentence. It was this which, it is said, inspired the expression 'to be lynched', but it must be a wildly devious derivation, as the crowd in fact wanted to save Walter, not hang him.

Galway's Catholic cathedral whose full name is **Cathedral of Our Lady Assumed into Heaven and St Nicholas** – has a giant dome looming over the city. The classical architecture is misleading; the church was dedicated in 1965.

Alongside the cathedral is Galway's **Salmon Weir**, in which the salmon fight their way from the sea up to the lakeland. From June to July you can see them queueing up for a chance to leap up the falls and follow their instincts to sweet water.

In Galway you can also visit the restored house of **Bowling Green**, the one-up, one-down dwelling where James Joyce's, wife, Nora Barnacle, lived and was brought up.

Galway's seaside suburb, **Salthill**, is a hugely popular resort with many rocky sea-walls and beaches of fine sand, which are ideal for a walk. It's a great place to watch the sun set on Galway Bay; sprawling hills enclose almost all of this immense bay, but the Atlantic Ocean can be seen and sensed to the west.

CONNEMARA AND THE ARAN ISLANDS

Lough Corrib, which extends 27 miles (43km) north from Galway, is big enough to be whipped by waves when the sudden wind hurtles down the hillside. It's generally shallow and well supplied with islands and fish – salmon, trout, pike and perch. Lough Corrib divides County Galway into two contrasting regions: to the east a fertile limestone plain, and to the west Connemara, a range of dramatic mountains and a series of sparkling lake, all enclosed by the coastline of fjords and pristine beaches.

Much of Connemara is an Irish-speaking enclave. This is the home of the Connemara pony – robust, intelligent and self-reliant. Spanish horses of the 16th century are rumoured to have cross-bred with Irish ponies: one version says that the stallions swam ashore from ships of the Spanish Armada wrecked on nearby rocks.

The sky seems to change by the minute in the far west – dazzling sun, fleeting clouds and rain alternating so quickly that photographers have to be constantly at the ready. But the resulting photos are definitely worth the effort in a land of thatched, white, stone cottages and 180-degree rainbows.

The so-called 'capital' is the well-placed market town of **Clifden**, a base for exploring the nearby lakes and rivers, as well as fine beaches, bogs and mountains. The town's Irish name is *An Clochan*, meaning 'Stepping Stones'. There are in fact so many areas of water around Clifden that you can't tell the genuine sea inlets from the coves of the lakes, except for the seaweed, a plant which incidentally also features often in Irish cooking.

Killary Harbour, near Lee-nane, offers superb anchorage which is protected by very high mountain walls on both sides. The floats and rafts, which look as if they belong to an oil project, are actually busy with farming ever-popular mussels.

Funnily enough, the Irish don't think much of seafood, so it is generally exported to France where there are more true seafood enthusiasts.

From Bog to Stove

In this energy-hungry world it sounds too good to be true: you go to a field, dig up the moist topsoil, dry it, and then burn it for cooking, heating the house, even generating electricity. Of course, in real life it's not so easy, but peat, the typically Irish fuel, does produce about half the heat of coal.

Locally known as turf, peat is found in the bogs which cover one-sixth of the country. It is created by centuries of interaction between the bog's water and vegetable matter. After the bog is drained, the turf is cut into uniform chunks, stacked for drying, and eventually collected for use. A typical family burns 12 to 15 tonnes a year.

Now city slickers can even buy peat briquettes to burn in their fireplaces to create the sweet nostalgic smell of Ireland.

93

The huge **Twelve Bens** of Connemara (*ben* is Gaelic for 'peak') constitute a range of moody mountains which are inhabited mostly by sheep; the foothills are interspersed with bogs and pretty lakes.

Now for some real escapism. Out in the Atlantic, 30 miles (48km) off Galway, the **Aran Islands** are a last bastion of peace and quiet and unbroken tradition. Their tall, handsome population, with strong, open faces, survive on a land so harsh that every blade of grass seems a miracle. They raise sturdy cattle, catch fish, and spin, weave and knit. Aran sweaters are sold all over the country, but only here can you be sure it's the genuine, handmade article.

Inishmore, 'the Big Island' as the Aran folk call it, is about 9 miles (14km) from tip to tip and only 2 miles (3km) across. From the air – and you can fly there from Galway – you see a tight gridwork of stone fences enclosing pockets of meagre pasture. In some fields you can even see the rock just beneath the grass.

Inishmore's one and only real village, **Kilronan**, has a port where ferryboats from the mainland dock. The fishermen work aboard modern trawlers, but the traditional *currachs* are still used. These tar-coated, canvas-hulled boats, made by hand, now enjoy the power of outboard motors.

This is an island to explore on foot or rented bicycle. If you're in a hurry, you can hire pony-traps for guided tours, or the island even has a single motorized taxi which doubles as a school bus.

The most remarkable monument here is **Dun Aengus**, a giant prehistoric fortress on the sheer edge of a cliff some 300ft (91m) high. It's about a 15-minute walk from the road, across unobtrusively marked fields. Three layers of stone walls, the outermost 20ft (6m) high, surround the courtyard 150ft (46m) across. With the ramparts and obstacles set up beyond the wall, the total area covers 11 acres (4ha). Even in modern times it would take a rash General to stage an attack on Dun Aengus.

Elsewhere on the islands, among the colourful, delicate wild flowers, grazing cows and sheep, and an abundance of bounding rabbits, there are numerous **archaeological sites**, which are of less importance, but which nevertheless have their own diversion to offer. Here you'll find stone forts and groups of primitive stone dwellings, as well as hermits' cells, round towers and several ruined churches.

In striking contrast to these and other similarly traditional structures, a big glass-walled factory situated in the west of Inishmore exports its products to many corners of the world where they are in demand. The time-honoured dexterity of the Aran women has been fully diverted from the local, hardy wool to wire; nowadays they weave telephone cables and make electronic components. The language they all speak is Irish, but most people on the islands can also speak English. Whether they greet you with '*Failte*' or 'Welcome', they will all have a friendly greeting for strangers.

COUNTY MAYO

Rising high above Clew Bay, **Croagh Patrick** is Ireland's Holy Mountain. With so many appealing mountains, this holy peak looks more like a black slag heap. Even so, thousands of pilgrims climb the slopes to the imposing summit.

The thousands of pilgrims who climb Croagh Patrick – Ireland's Holy Mountain – are rewarded with stunning views.

St Patrick is said to have spent Lent here in 441. There are views of the bay and the hills of counties Mayo, Clare and Galway.

The town of **Westport**, at the head of Clew Bay, is an example of 18th-century urban planning. The Mall boulevard follows the Carrowbeg River, and the town's main plaza is an elegant octagon.

Outside the town, the home of the Marquess of Sligo can be visited from April to October. **Westport House** is palatial, with paintings, silver and glassware. There's a souvenir shop, go-cart rides for children and even a dungeon.

Inland, the village of **Knock** (from the Irish *Cnoc Mhuire* – 'Mary's Hill') is a respected place of pilgrimage. In 1879 the townsfolk saw an apparition of the Virgin Mary, St Joseph and St John on a south gable of the old parish church. The centenary year reached its climax when the pilgrim Pope John Paul II came from Rome to address an open-air mass at Knock with at least 400,000 of the faithful.

Getting there is easy now that the international airport is in operation. Knock also caters to the pilgrims: there are souvenir shops, and a museum of folklore and handicrafts.

A new **basilica** – Ireland's biggest church – was built in advance of the anniversary; it can hold 20,000 worshippers. The small parish church is still there, but the **south gable** had to be restored after much of the mortar was taken away as relics. The site of the famous apparition has been enclosed in glass, and statues re-create the position of the figures in the vision.

In the town of **Foxford**, a new interpretative centre tells the story of the old woollen mills and the famine in the area, while near Ballycastle, on the north Mayo cliffs, the new pyramid-shaped heritage centre of **Ceide Fields** reveals the ancient history of the many prehistoric settlements in the area. The site is estimated to be the single largest Stone Age monument in existence in the the world today. It dates as far back as 3000 BC.

Achill, the country's biggest island, is buffeted by wind and tide, with meagre farms between ominous mountains and rocky shores. It feels adrift, though you can drive there from the mainland across a short and unimpressive bridge.

Driving on Achill's wide open and deserted roads can revive the joy of motoring. But even if the traffic were heavy, the truly magnificent scenery – from 800ft (244m) cliffs to superb beaches – would still be worth the trouble.

Near the modest village of Keel, **Trawmore Strand** is an outstanding model of a long, white-sand beach. Keel's large nine-hole golf course spreads to the dunes and so suffers no shortage of bunkers.

Prehistoric graves can be found on the harsh slopes of Achill's overpoweringly high mountain, the 2,204ft (672m) **Slievemore**. Driving offers the most dizzying cliff views and perspectives from the ocean churning round the off-islands and shoals. Inland, note the three-chimneyed cottages set between moors and bogs.

The North West

Sligo (population 18,000) lies between two mountains: Ben Bulben and Knocknarea.

Early fame came to Sligo in 807 when the Vikings invaded. In 1252 Maurice Fitzgerald, the Earl of Kildare, founded **Sligo Abbey**, a Dominican friary. It was accidentally burnt down in 1414, but rebuilt soon afterwards. Then it suffered an attack by Puritan troops in 1641, and the friars were killed. Its ruins combine desolation with grace. Three sides have been preserved, and there are excellent carvings.

The resort **Strandhill**, west of Sligo, has a beach with long-rolling waves for surfers. **Knocknarea**, the flat-topped mountain over this stretch of shore, must have had a strange attraction for the early settlers.

The area has an abundance of megalithic monuments and on the 1,078ft (329m) summit of Knocknarea there is a *cairn* (tomb of stones). Legend says it is the burial place of the first-century Queen Maeve of Connaught.

*B*en Bulben mountain, County Sligo, looms over WB Yeats' grave in Drumcliff churchyard.

Facing Strandhill, on the opposite side of the harbour, are the resorts of Rosses Point and **Coney Island**, after which, it is said, New York's amusement park was named.

WB Yeats is buried near the front door of the town's small **98** church, with its turreted belfry in the shadow of the awesome **Ben Bulben**, 1,730ft (527m) high. On its flat top you'll find arctic and alpine plants.

About 17 miles (27km) to the north of Sligo, situated on the approach to the village of Mullaghmore, look out for the stunning **Classiebawn Castle**, which claims the skyline all to itself. This was the summer dwelling of Earl Mountbatten of Burma, who was assassinated by the IRA in 1979 when his fishing boat was blown up just off the shore nearby.

COUNTY DONEGAL

The most northerly county on the island, Donegal is known for its scenery – mountains glens and lakes. This is where the Donegal homespun **tweed** comes from.

Donegal's medieval **castle** occupies the site of a previous Viking fort. (*Dun na nGall* in Irish means the 'Fortress of the Foreigners', a reference to the Vikings.) On the edge of town, the ruins of Donegal Abbey overlook the estuary.

Westward along the coast, **Killybegs** is a really big-time fishing port; the trawlers have wheelhouses with devices for tracking down the fish.

The road to the village of **Glencolumbkille** heads deep into spectacular country. Over the crest of a hill, you see the simple village below, enfolded in green hillsides that funnel down to the sea. In Irish the name Glencolumbkille means the 'Glen of St Colmcille' (or St Columba). Today it is said that the 6th-century saint, who changed the course of history by introducing the Christian faith to Scotland, began his career by converting locals. The numerous old **standing-stones** were formerly pagan monuments which St Columba simply adapted to the new religion. On the saint's feast day, 9 June, pilgrims follow the pathway of these old stones. Over 40 prehistoric *dolmens*, *souterrains* and *cairns* have been catalogued in this area, some as old as 5,000 years.

Set between Derry and Letterkenny, you can visit the **stone fort** built in prehistoric times, which is well-preserved and similar in style to Staigue Fort in Co Kerry (see p.81). Fort Dunree on the Inishowen peninsula overlooking Lough Swilly is a fascinating military history museum in an old fort.

Glenveagh National Park forms 24,710 acres (10,000ha) of the most beautiful part of Co Donegal, including Glenveagh Castle and Glebe House which was built in 1828 in graceful Regency style and sumptuously furnished. It was once the home of Derek Hill, the artist, who gave it to the Irish nation.

99

Northern Ireland

The Union Jack flies over six of the nine counties forming the ancient province of Ulster, a fact which stirs fiery feelings in the Irish people.

Unarguably the sectarian violence of recent years has affected daily life in Northern Ireland: the centre of Belfast has been turned into a pedestrian mall by default, now surrounded by a stern security cordon. However, the scenery of exuberant rolling hills, with its lovely lakes, and a grandiose coast, remains unscathed.

Here are the main attractions of Northern Ireland:

The **Antrim Coast Road** is a marvel of the 19th-century skills in technical engineering. It hugs an impressively scenic coastline, beneath white cliffs, beside beaches, through quaint villages and craggy rockfaces showing the geological history of our planet in many facets.

The seascapes to be seen here may be splendid, but the nine idyllic **Glens of Antrim** along the way, with their many green forests, dancing water-falls and streams, are the stuff of legends.

One of the candidates for the title 'eighth wonder of the world', the **Giant's Causeway** is Ireland's most amazing natural phenomenon. Molten lava was frozen into some 38,000 basalt columns, most of which are hexagonal, and these form the tightly packed 'stepping stones' out into the sea. This vast, spectacular oddity, some 60 million years old, excites the imagination of even the most cynical observer. Some of the individual formations even have names like the Honeycomb, the Chimney Pots and the Wishing Chair.

Nearby at **Port na Spaniagh**, a Spanish Armada ship was wrecked in 1588. Nearly four centuries later Belgian divers recovered an incredible king's ransom in gold, silver and jewels, the best of which are now on view at the Ulster Museum in Belfast.

Ulster's indefatigable statisticians can't say how many lakes there are in **County Fermanagh**, but they have counted an astonishing 154 islands in the 50-mile (80km) stretch of Upper and Lower Lough Erne. 'Fisherman's paradise' is the appropriate subtitle for Fermanagh, and no wonder – in 1979, a now famous angler named Dennis Willis managed to pull in an incredible 207 lbs (93kg) of fish in a period of just five hours. Millions more roach, pike, perch and bream are still available on this shore, and there is no closed season on coarse fishing.

In Northern Ireland's most imposing range, compact but aloof, the 15 granite peaks of the **Mourne Mountains** tower more than 2,000ft (610m) over the land below. At the summit of Slieve Donard you will find two *cairns* (ancient mounds of stones). From here, on a flawless day, you can see Scotland, England, the Isle of Man and Snowdonia in Wales.

Much livelier than its name might indicate to visitors, the **Ulster Folk and Transport Museum** enjoys a grand total of 172 acres (70ha) of the greenest woodland park. Old farmhouses, mills and even a church were all moved with painstaking labour, stone by stone, from their original sites all over Ulster to be preserved in one spot – the agricultural, industrial and social history of the province. In the transport section you can admire ancient carriages and bicycles, as well as cars and aircraft. Another museum in Cultra Manor, in County Down, is only about 8 miles (13km) from Belfast.

Ulster Museum, a modern site in Belfast itself, also looks out onto a beautiful park, the Botanic Gardens.

The art department features Irish and British painting up to the present day, while the archaeological exhibits begin with prehistoric Irish artefacts and continue through to working relics of the Industrial Revolution which transformed Belfast from the village it was then to the metropolis it is nowadays.

Navan Fort, near Armagh, is one of the most important Celtic sites in Europe and was the seat of the ancient kings of Ulster. It offers a stunning visual and interactive display which children will enjoy. **101**

What to Do

Sports

Whether by land or sea (or river or lake) the Irish enjoy so many sporting possibilities that for we can only touch on a handful of the big favourites. If you are interested in more esoteric sports, such as hang-gliding, orienteering or even polo, the tourist board can put you in touch with the appropriate sports associations.

SPORTS ON THE WATER

Sailing: any seasoned old salt with a seaworthy yacht will no doubt welcome the challenges of the west coast, but first-time sailors will be better off handling conditions off the south and east coasts and in the bays all around the island. Ask the tourist board for details about boat hire and sailing tuition.

Sea fishing: any way you like it – from a long sandy beach, a **102** pier, a clifftop or a boat – you too can hook big beautiful trophies of the deep: shark, sea bass, tope, skate, halibut, conger and many more.

Swimming: the tourist board's information sheet on seaside resorts lists a dozen – not bad for such a modestly sized island. The beaches come in all shapes and sizes, but have one thing in common: no crowds.

Surfing: the heavy Atlantic swells are more impressive on the west and north coasts, and so offer better surfing.

Boating: cruising on a river is very popular. You can also try more energetic sports such as canoeing on lakes, or rivers.

Game fishing: fertile salmon fisheries are mostly restricted, but arrangements can be made – though preferably well in advance. Trout are abundant in rivers and lakes; as with salmon, you will need a licence.

Coarse fishing: free almost everywhere, all year, and with huge catches.

SPORTS ASHORE

Golf: in a country so green, you might scarcely notice the vast number of golf courses, but there are an amazing 300, including several which are of championship status. There are at least 40 further courses currently under construction in the Republic, and while you will find non-members may be excluded over the weekend, you'll have no problems on weekdays.

In between rounds you can always keep in shape with pitch and putt, a traditional Irish game somewhere between minigolf and the real thing, played with a putter and one other club.

Greyhound racing: this is a very popular pursuit on the island. Teams of hare-brained dogs keep eager punters busy six nights a week in Dublin –

which has two greyhound stadiums – and elsewhere.

Horse racing: almost everyone in Ireland seems to be totally engrossed, one way or another, in the Sport of Kings. Dublin boasts two tracks, and several famous courses within easy reach on a day-trip. The flat season is from March to November, and steeple-chase racing goes on all year.

Horse riding: stables can be found all over Ireland with fine Irish horses, beautiful ponies,

*R*oss Carberry is one of the many picturesque villages along the stunning coastline of Cork.

Ireland is the perfect place for golf enthusiasts, with more golf courses per capita than any other European country.

and trekking routes through delightful verdant countryside.

Tennis: many hotels advertise their own courts, some of them with instructors, but elsewhere there are public courts, as in many Dublin parks.

National games: hurling is a very fast variant of hockey, in which a small, leather-covered ball is struck with a 'hurley', similar to a hockey stick.

Gaelic football, that other very traditional Irish game, includes elements of both soccer and rugby.

Imported games: athletics, soccer, rugby and even cricket are also widely played.

104

Shopping

Friendly sales staff help make shopping in Ireland a real pleasure. Shopkeepers are so sincere here that they'll advertise a competitor if they think they are selling something better.

The appealing products here are made by Irish craftsmen in traditional or imaginative new styles. Here are some ideas:

Aran sweaters: the elaborate stitches in these fishermen's sweaters can be easily recognized. Demand so far exceeds the supply that they are now made in mainland factories as well as in the cottages on the Aran islands. Look at the label to find out if it is hand-knitted.

Connemara marble: a rich green, this stone is made into all kinds of souvenirs.

Crafts: an array of enamel dishes, plaques and pendants by local craftsmen.

Crosses: reproductions of old Christian crosses, and pretty St Brigid crosses of straw.

Dolls: dressed in traditional regional costumes.

Glassware: Waterford crystal, world renowned, is once again a busy concern. Crystal is also produced in Tipperary, Cavan, Dublin, Galway and Tyrone.

Jewellery: Celtic designs and illustrations from the Book of Kells inspire some of today's goldsmiths and silversmiths.

Kinsale smocks: these hardy cotton wind-cheaters are made for local sailors – not to be confused with Kinsale cloaks, traditional dress now revived as chic evening-wear.

Lace: nuns in Limerick and County Monaghan have kept this industry alive.

Linen: weaving continues in Northern Ireland, but the end product – from handkerchiefs upwards – is sold everywhere.

Paintings: many Irish-based artists produce fine studies of Ireland, including landscapes, seascapes, flora and fauna, in oils, watercolours and pen and wash. These works are widely available and well priced.

Peat: even the turf of Ireland is now compressed and sculpted into reproductions of ancient religious and mythical folklore symbols.

Pottery: both traditional and modern designs in tableware and ovenware.

Rushwork: in a land rich with thatched cottages, the makers of woven baskets and similar wickerwork are still working in a thriving business.

Smoked salmon: a souvenir you can eat that is specially packed for travelling, and on sale at the airport.

Souvenirs: leprechauns in all sizes, pretty 'worry stones' of marble, as well as elegant Irish coffee glasses and *shillelaghs* (cudgels) are all widely available. Books, published in Ireland, about every aspect of Irish life and its history, make easy-to-carry souvenirs.

Tweed: handwoven fabrics in a variety of bright and subtle colours and weights, ideal for overcoats, jackets, drapes or light shawls.

Nightlife

Many hotels and pubs present **cabaret nights** featuring the most diverse cross-section of traditional Irish entertainment possible: folk singers, harpists, dancers and storytellers. In local pubs the programme may consist of a lone folk singer with guitar. At the other end of the scale the luxury hotels put on elaborate productions with a host of performers.

The shows have a typically Irish mixture of hand-clapping high spirits and 'Come Back to Erin' nostalgia. Jigs and reels are tirelessly danced, and lively tap dancers revive some of the country's oldest and best routines. Harps and banjos are plucked and bagpipes and accordions squeezed. Fast fiddlers are as ubiquitous here as gypsy violinists in Budapest, though a lot more cheerful.

Ireland abounds in traditional music, song and dance – as the song says: 'Come dance with me in Ireland.'

You will find less polished versions of traditional Irish music at *fleadhanna*, festivals of music and song around the country, climaxing in the all Ireland *Fleadh* in the summer (August). Tourist offices will have detailed schedules.

Dublin has a lively **nightclub** scene, with music for all tastes. Lower Leeson Street, the leading nightspot, has become somewhat passé with newer venues in the city centre along the many quays becoming more appealing to younger crowds seeking lively entertainment. The more up-to-date nightclubs usually offer witty and fast-talking DJs or other artistes, food, drink, and very often a celebrity or two from the worlds of film and music.

Restored medieval castles are used for another kind of night out – grandiose candlelit **banquets** with traditional stories, poems and songs. These re-creations of lusty celebrations from the past are professionally arranged. If you have no car you can join package tours which include door-to-door transportation.

Ireland's grand **theatrical** tradition – which gave the world Goldsmith, Shaw, Sheridan, Becket, O'Casey and Behan – continues in some major towns such as Dublin, Belfast and Cork. The Abbey Theatre, Dublin is still 'packing them in' after more than 75 years. Newspapers usually print full listings of theatrical events as well as concerts and films.

CALENDAR OF EVENTS

As dates frequently change, we advise you to contact the local tourist office for up-to-date information on particular festivals.

March: *St Patrick's Week* – parades and many other events in Dublin and various towns.

April: *The Cork International Choral Festival.*
The famous *Irish Grand National* horse race.

May: *Cork International Choral and Folk Dance Festival.*
Dublin Spring Show and Industries Fair.
Killarney Pan-Celtic Week – competitions and cultural events which enjoy the participation of other Celtic countries.
Listowel Writers Week – taking place in County Kerry.

June: *Festival of Music* staged in great Irish houses.
Dundalk Maytime Festival – classical music in great Irish houses.

July: *International Folk Dance Festival* – held in Cobh.
Dun Laoghaire Festival – held in County Dublin.
Galway Arts Festival and horse races.
Irish Open Golf Champonships.

August: *Dublin Horse Show* – the top event of the year.
Connemara Pony Show – held in Clifden, County Galway.
Kilkenny Arts Week.
Moynalty Steam Threshing Fair – held in County Meath.
Puck Fair – three days and nights of non-stop Irish entertainment), Killorglin, Co. Kerry.
Stradbally Steam Rally – staged in County Laois.

September: *National Football and Hurling Finals* – Dublin.
Festival of Light Opera – staged in Waterford.
Rose of Tralee Festival – an international event (see p.82).

October: *Kinsale Gourmet Festival* – staged in County Cork.
Dublin Theatre Festival (Dublin) – new plays by Irish authors and companies from abroad.
Cork International Film Festival.
Wexford Opera Festival, shows of rare operas.
Ballinasloe Fair (Europe's oldest horse fair), County Galway.
Cork Jazz Festival.

November: *The International Horse Show* (Dublin) – a classic event of the Royal Dublin Society, and one of the major occasions on the international equestrian calendar.

Children in Ireland

Fun activities for children of all ages can be found at:

Bray promenade, 12 miles (19km) south of Dublin. A big seaside resort with dodgems, and a seafront aquarium.

Captain Venture, Level 3, The Square, Tallaght, Dublin 22, tel. (01) 459 6039. Amusements for children up to 13.

Clara-Lara, Vale of Clara, County Wicklow, tel. (0404) 46161. Fun park, trout farm and amusements for children.

Dublin Zoo, tel. (01) 677 1425. A wide variety of animals, from elephants to polar bears. Café and restaurant.

Farm visits. In numerous regions farms are open to visitors and offer a warm welcome to children. Tourist information offices have full details.

Fota Island, near the town of Cobh, Co. Cork, tel. (021) 812 678. Large wildlife park, open March-October.

Fun Factory, Monkstown, Co. Dublin, tel. (01) 284 3344. An activity centre for children up to the age of 12.

Irish National Heritage Centre, near Wexford, tel. (053) 41733. Full-sized replicas of buildings from prehistoric to Norman times. Open all year.

Kilmainhaim Jail, Dublin, tel. (01) 453 5984. An historic jail converted into a history and heritage centre. Open all year, every day.

Museum of Childhood, Dublin 6, tel. (01) 497 3223. A fascinating collection of dolls and dolls' houses as far back as the early 18th century.

National Gallery of Ireland, Merrion Square West, Dublin 2, tel. (01) 661 5133. Frequent children's activities.

National Wax Museum, off Parnell Square, Dublin 1, tel. (01) 872 6340. Realistic wax **109**

figures as well as a Chamber of Horrors.

Newbridge Demesne, County Dublin, tel. (01) 843 6534. An 18th-century house with farm and animals.

Straffan Steam Museum, in County Kildare, tel. (01) 628 8412, has model and full-sized steam engines. Open all year.

The **butterfly farm** has a large number of butterflies as well as hairy tarantulas and other poisonous spiders. Open in summer months only.

Tralee, in Co. Kerry. Steam train runs from the town to Blennerville, a restored early 19th-century windmill only 2 miles away.

Westport House, Westport, Co. Mayo, tel. (098) 25430. Play facilities for children, a zoo, and a steam railway.

Children and adults alike will enjoy a day out at Sandycove Beach, close to the Joyce Tower Museum.

Eating Out

Like most Anglo-Saxons, the Irish prefer 'honest' meat and potatoes heaped high on their plates – they are no fans of the esoteric sauces and spices of European cuisines.

In Ireland, if you should ask someone to recommend a restaurant, the main criterion is most likely to be quantity rather than quality. Even so, you can hardly go wrong when it comes to ingredients. The abundance of fresh meat, fish, butter and eggs does go a long way to compensate for the lack of *haute cuisine* in most Irish restaurants.

Hearty meals are served in a baffling array of places – from hotels and bars to coffee shops and snack bars, from pubs to restaurants. 'Pub grub' tends to be hot or cold meat pies, sandwiches and simple salads, while restaurants run from the most modest to the truly elegant, with prices to match. There are now also ever more foreign restaurants, especially in the larger towns.

Keep in mind the 'business-man's lunch', a package deal found in many provincial and city restaurants, which usually involves a set three courses for a fraction of the cost of an evening meal. This is worth considering if you are travelling with a limited budget.

In addition to VAT (value added tax), a lot of restaurants add a service charge to the bill; extra tips are rare.

WHEN TO EAT

Breakfast is served from about 7 to 10am, though in some hotels, matching the general leisurely air, it doesn't begin until 8am. Lunchtime is from 12.30 to 2.30pm, give or take half an hour at either end.

The hour – and name – of the evening meal depends on who and where you are. In rural areas and perhaps the less sophisticated town areas, people dine as early as 6pm and refer to the evening meal as 'tea'. In the major towns and cities, however, you can have your 'supper' any time from 6 or 7 to 11pm.

WHAT TO EAT

Breakfast

A real Irish breakfast starts the day superlatively. You'll feel ready for any kind of exertion after a menu of juice, porridge or cold cereal with milk or cream, fried eggs with bacon and sausages, toast or tasty home-made soda bread, butter, marmalade, tea or coffee. Irish soda bread, white or brown, is made from flour and butter-milk, bicarbonate of soda and salt; it's as delicious as cake.

Other meals

Irish **soups** are usually thick and hearty: vegetables, barley and meat stock with a dab of cream, for instance. Look for potato soup made of potatoes, onions, carrot and parsley.

Fish caught fresh from the Atlantic, the Irish Sea or the island's streams is incredibly good. The Irish, however, are unenthusiastic about almost all kinds of seafood, presumably because of a mental block –
112 until recent years Catholics

were obliged to abstain from meat on Fridays, so fish was thought of as a poor substitute. Keep an eye out anyway for some of these great Irish delights: fresh salmon (poached or grilled), smoked salmon, sole and trout from the sea and rivers. Dublin Bay prawns are a big natural resource worthy of their fame, as are Galway oysters (often accompanied by a bottle of stout). With luck you could be offered mussels or lobster, but the great bulk of the catch is usually exported to the Continent.

Meat of the highest quality is at the centre of Irish cuisine. The beef is excellent, but there is very little veal. You'll have a choice of sumptuous steaks (either T-bone, filet mignon or sirloin) or roast beef. Lamb appears as tender chops or as a roast, or the main ingredient in Irish stew, a filling casserole of meat, potatoes, carrots and onions, laced with parsley and thyme. Irish pork products – bacon, sausages, chops, and Limerick ham – are also rightly famous. Dublin Coddle is a delicious stew of sausages, bacon, onions, potatoes and parsley, a favourite for Saturday night supper in the capital.

Vegetables as basic as the potato play a big part in Irish cooking. Potatoes have been a mainstay of the Irish diet since the 17th century. Mushrooms, which thrive in a cool, humid atmosphere here, are the single biggest horticultural export. More and more restaurants are now serving vegetarian dishes.

Desserts are often similar to sticky English 'puddings' – trifles, gateaux and generally very sweet offerings, sometimes with a scrumptious topping of thick cream.

WHAT TO DRINK

A pitcher of tap **water** is often found on the table, and for many diners it's the only drink during the meal. Ireland has about half-a-dozen brands of bottled spring water, widely sold and served in pubs and restaurants, and it is gaining popularity as a substitute for alcoholic drinks, especially at lunchtime. Some people prefer milk instead of alcohol, and wine is becoming popular in Ireland as links with Europe strengthen. By a quirk in the law, restaurants licensed to serve sherry and wine cannot serve spirits or beer, but the Irish don't see beer as a dinner accompaniment anyway.

Pubs such as the Lord Edward in Dublin stand tall and proud, part of the Irish heritage.

Irish **pubs** are usually as relaxed and friendly as their regular clients. Although the eccentric licensing hours used to mean that public houses in the Republic's urban areas had to close between 2.30 and 3.30pm, this 'holy hour' no longer exists, and most pubs are open all day, but they are still closed on Sunday afternoons. The pubs in Northern Ireland are permitted to open on Sundays, but not all choose to do so.

The Irish drink nearly 500 million pints of **beer** a year, mostly stout – a rich, creamy, dark brown version. Cork's two brands of stout, Beamish and Murphy's, are becoming increasingly popular.

In many a pub the simple order 'a pint, please' means 568 millilitres of **Guinness**, lovingly drawn from the keg and scraped and topped. The 'head' is so thick the barman can sculpt it with his spatula like a baker icing a cake. A 'glass' of stout means half a pint. Irish lagers and ales are much less filling, and are also **114** worth trying.

An interesting Irish drink, **Black Velvet**, combines stout and champagne, and is thought to be good for a hangover.

The word **whiskey** comes from the Gaelic *uisce beatha*, 'water of life'. (Purists are at pains to spell Irish whiskey with an 'e', unlike the Scottish version). Whiskey is matured in wooden casks for at least seven years and is drunk neat, or with a little water – never with ice. Enthusiasts can visit the world's oldest whiskey distillery, Bushmills, in Northern Ireland, which has held a license since 1609.

Whiskey figures in some unusual drinks: **Irish Coffee**, in a stemmed glass, is hot coffee laced with whiskey and sugar, with a tablespoonful of thick cream floating on top. Two Irish liqueurs merit a try: **Irish Mist** – honey and herbs in a whiskey base – tingles on the palate, and **Irish Cream Liqueur**, in different brands: there's Bailey's and Carolan's, Sheridan's and St Brendan's. It contains whiskey, chocolate and cream, like a leprechaun's milkshake.

BLUEPRINT
for a
Perfect Trip

An A–Z Summary of Practical Information

Certain items of information printed in this section will already be familiar to residents of Ireland, but have been included for visitors from overseas.

A

ACCOMMODATIONS (See also CAMPING on p.118, YOUTH HOSTELS on p.141 and the selection of RECOMMENDED HOTELS starting on p.65)

While exploring Ireland you can stay in a varied combination of different accommodations: a super-luxury hotel one night, a family-run guest house the next, a farmhouse and a thatched cottage after that. Efficient tourist offices will handle both spur-of-the-moment or long-range reservations for you. The tourist boards are responsible for inspecting and classifying all hostelries, issuing brochures free or at minimal cost, and for listing the various approved establishments available with information about their rates and facilities. Tariffs are government-controlled, and the maximum rate shown in the brochure is the highest which proprietors may charge.

Hotel bills usually include a service charge, and you will find that VAT (value added tax) on the total cost of accommodation, meals and service is included in the tariffs.

Hotels and motor hotels. These are graded by the tourist authorities into five different categories:

A*: most luxurious with high standard of cuisine and services.

116 A: extremely comfortable with experienced service.

B*: well-furnished, offering a good service; a private bath available but not necessarily in the majority of rooms.
B: well-kept, limited but good cuisine and service.
C: clean and comfortable, hot and cold running water.
Hotels and motels, which are newly built and therefore too new to have been classified, are listed ungraded.

Guesthouses. Usually family-run with friendly personal service, these can include full board for resident guests, and are also listed and graded. Make sure that you enquire prior to booking about the full services offered.

Irish Homes. The Irish Tourist Board issues *Guest Accommodation*, a weighty and informative book covering a full range of hotels, guesthouses and youth hostels, as well as town and country homes, and farmhouses. The Northern Ireland Tourist Board publishes two similar brochures, *Where to Stay* and *Farm and Country Holidays*. As for finding Bed and Breakfast accommodation, you don't need any brochures to find them – you'll see signs all over the place.

Thatched Cottages. This scheme operates mainly in western Ireland near famous beauty spots in five counties. The details are available from tourist offices or Rent-an-Irish Cottage Ltd, Shannon Free Airport, Co. Clare; tel. (061) 61588.

AIRPORTS

International flights arrive at five airports, in the east, south, west and north: Dublin, Cork, Shannon, Knock and Belfast.

Dublin Airport, 7 miles (11km) north of the capital, is the busiest. Coaches link the airport with Busaras, the city bus terminal, every 20 minutes. The trip takes about half an hour. Taxi time between the airport and central Dublin is also about half an hour.

Dublin Airport has all the amenities that international travellers look for, including a porter service and push-it-yourself trolleys. Rounding off these facilities are a bank, car-hire desks, a church, hairdresser, nursery, post and tourist information offices, as well as a hotel-reservation desk, bars, restaurants and shops, including a duty-free shop, and duty-free facilities for incoming passengers. **117**

Shannon Airport, one of the first Atlantic gateways, is situated about 15 miles (24km) to the west of Limerick. All usual facilities are available, as well as a vast and varied duty-free shopping area.

Belfast Airport (Aldergrove) is 15 miles (24km) west of the city centre. There is a coach service into town every 80 minutes.

B

·BICYCLE RENTAL (See also MONEY MATTERS on p.130)

A network of dealers all over the island encourages bike rental as a way of seeing 'the real Ireland'. Children's and adults' models, racing bikes and even tandems are all available. Tourist information offices have a leaflet listing dealers in more than 100 towns from Antrim to Cork. Motorbikes and mopeds cannot be hired in Ireland.

C

CAMPING (See also MONEY MATTERS on p.130)

Officially-approved campsites range from spartan to luxurious, but if a 'no vacancy' sign is posted, take heart: many a farmer will let campers spend the night on his property, but you should always ask first. At some campsites, and at rental agencies, touring caravans (trailers) can be hired. If you're pulling your own, note that the connections for Calor gas tanks are not suitable for the cylinders sold in Ireland. Lists of camping and caravanning parks and their various facilities are available from tourist information offices or the Irish Caravan Council, 2 Offington Court, Sutton, Dublin 13; tel. (01) 323776. Contact the Northern Ireland Tourist Board at St Anne's Court, North Street, Belfast BT1 1ND; tel. (0232) 231221.

Horse-drawn caravans may be hired by the week, if you want to get a taste of the gipsy life. They are most commonly found in the west and south west of Ireland. Bookings should be made in advance through the Central Reservation Service, Irish Tourist Board, Baggot **118** Street Bridge, Dublin 2; tel. (01) 676 58 71.

CAR RENTAL (See also DRIVING IN IRELAND on p.122 and MONEY MATTERS on p.130)

Dozens of car rental companies operate at airports and in the towns, dealing in everything from minicars to so-called executive cars and vans. The internationally known firms usually have slightly higher rates than their local competitors, but you may find that booking from abroad might get you better value for money. Some companies permit cars to be picked up in one place and handed in elsewhere.

Most companies have a two-tiered tariff, raising prices by up to 10 to 20 percent for the summer season. In any season, cars may be rented on a 'time-plus-mileage' basis or with unlimited mileage, but if you're unsure whether you'll be chalking up enough travelling to justify the 'unlimited' rate, the firm may agree to let you choose the more favourable tariff retroactively. Investigate before you travel.

A valid national licence, normally at least two years old, will be required. Many firms permit 21-year-old drivers to rent cars, but the minimum age can be as high as 25. The maximum age, depending on the company, ranges from 65 to 70. Credit cards are normally accepted in lieu of a deposit.

Rental rates include third-party liability insurance. Additional coverage can be arranged on the spot, and comprehensive cover is recommended.

Don't forget: drive on the left and wear your seat belt at all times.

CLIMATE and CLOTHING

The Gulf Stream is credited with keeping the Irish weather mild all year round, but the unexpected can happen with readings as cold as -2°F (-19°C) and as hot as 92°F (33°C) recorded over the past century. May is usually the sunniest month of the year, and December the dullest.

Average monthly temperatures in Dublin:

	J	F	M	A	M	J	J	A	S	O	N	D
°F	41	41	43	47	51	56	59	58	56	50	45	43
°C	5	5	6	8	11	13	15	14	13	10	7	6

Temperatures do not vary much from north to south, but the weather in the west and south west can be a good deal more wet than elsewhere because the winds come in over the land direct from the sea, bringing moisture with them. It may be wise, therefore, to pack some light protective clothing for the summer, and certainly warmer items in the winter.

In the winter the Wicklow Mountains near Dublin, Donegal in the north west and County Kerry in the south west have heavy snowfalls, making the territory dangerous even for the most seasoned walkers and climbers. Therefore wear hardy, warm and protective clothing and follow the proper code by informing the hotel owners of your route and time of return – and take some provisions with you.

COMMUNICATIONS (See also TIME DIFFERENCES on p.135)

Post Offices. The Post operates all mail services offered in the Republic. Most mailboxes are pillar-shaped (a few antiques still have Queen Victoria's monogram on them), and are painted green. Most post offices are open from 9am to 5.30pm, but the main one – the historic General Post Office in O'Connell Street, Dublin – is open until 8pm six days a week, and 6.30pm on Sundays. Postcard shops and newsagents sometimes sell stamps too. In some areas a post office may be identified by a sign in Irish only – *Oifig an Phoist*.

If you don't know where you'll be staying, you can have mail sent to you 'poste restante' (general delivery) to any town. Letters sent 'poste restante' to the GPO in Dublin may be collected up to 8pm.

In Northern Ireland the postboxes are red. Note that Republic of Ireland stamps may not be used on mail posted in Northern Ireland and British stamps are invalid in the Republic.

Telegrams. In Ireland the traditional telegram has been replaced by the telemessage. Dial 196 and it will be delivered the next day. The telemessage is accepted at post offices, with similar delivery speed.

Telephones. Public telephones are found in post offices, hotels, and stores and on the street. In the Republic sentry-box booths – cream-with green trim – and modern aluminium and glass booths are increasingly used. They are marked in Gaelic, *Telefon*.

Instructions for operating coin telephones are usually given. For payphones throughout Ireland use 10p, 20p 50p and £1 coins for direct dialling of local, national and international calls. Many payphones use callcards, which can be bought from local post offices and shops. Operator assistance is available by dialling 10.

In Northern Ireland public telephones are found in metal and glass booths or yellow cubicles. They operate with 10p, 50p and £1 coins and phonecards. Do not deposit money until the connection has been made; a series of rapid pips will indicate when the machine is ready to accept your coins.

COMPLAINTS

Your first move, of course, should be to complain to the manager of the offending establishment. If this fails to give satisfaction, turn to your nearest tourist office.

Complaints in writing may be directed to the Customer Relations Section, the Irish Tourist Board, Baggot Street Bridge, Dublin 2; tel. (01) 284 4768, or the Northern Ireland Tourist Board, St Anne's Court, North Street, Belfast BT1 1ND; tel. (0232) 246609.

You could also contact the Consumers Association of Ireland Ltd, 45 Upper Mount Street, Dublin 2; (01) 661 2466.

CRIME (See also EMERGENCIES on p.126 and POLICE on p.133)

The Crime Prevention Office of the *Garda Siochana* (police) warns visitors to carry a minimum of cash and jewellery. Pickpockets do operate in stores and public places. Tourists who leave property unattended risk losses; so park in well-lit, busy areas and keeping valuables out of sight. Thefts from hotel rooms are rare.

CUSTOMS and ENTRY FORMALITIES

Citizens of many countries do not require visas. British travellers directly from Britain require no passport or identity card, but others should present valid documents. Visitors from infected countries will need proof of vaccinations. It is forbidden to import pornographic material or books listed by the Republic of Ireland government's censor. You may bring unlimited Irish currency into the country, but you may only take out up to 100 Irish pounds. Foreign currency brought in can be taken out, plus the equivalent of 500 Irish pounds (traveller's cheques excluded). This does not apply to people travelling between Ireland and Great Britain, the Channel Islands or the Isle of Man.

Residents of European countries with goods bought in the EU (formerly EC) not-tax free, can bring into the Republic 300 or 75 cigars or 400g tobacco plus 1.5l spirits and 5l wine. European residents with tax-free goods can bring in 200 cigarettes or 50 cigars or 250g tobacco plus 1l spirits and 2l wine. Residents of non-European countries can bring in 400 cigarettes or 100 cigars or 500g tobacco plus 1l and 2l wine.

Visitors from Australia can bring in 200 cigarettes or 250 cigars or 250g tobacco, plus 1l spirits and 1l wine. Canada: 200 cigarettes, 50 cigars and 900g tobacco, plus 1.1l spirits and 1.1l wine. New Zealand: 200 cigarettes or 50 cigars or 250 tobacco, plus 1.1l spirits and 4.5l wine. South Africa: 400 cigarettes, 50 cigars and 250g tobacco plus 1l spirits and 2l wine. United Kingdom: 200 cigarettes or 50 cigars or 250g tobacco plus 1l spirits and 2l wine. USA: 200 cigarettes, 100 cigars and a reasonable quantity of tobacco, plus 1l spirits and 1l wine.

The customs restrictions between the Republic and Northern Ireland are normally limited to animals and agricultural products. Motorists are likely to undergo security checks at the 20 approved border crossings and are warned that they should avoid unauthorized crossing points.

D

DRIVING IN IRELAND (See also CAR RENTAL on p.119 and EMERGENCIES on p.126)

Traffic moves on the left, though not all Irish drivers worry about this formality. Many motorists in Ireland receive their licences without having taken a test, which shows in their sometimes odd driving habits. But competent foreign drivers confused by the roadsigns (some in Gaelic only) can also be a hazard.

Importing your car. Be sure to have the registration papers and insurance coverage. The usual formula is the Green Card, which is an extension to the normal insurance, making it valid in other countries. Your car should also have a nationality plate on the back. Virtually any valid driving licence from any country is recognized in Ireland.

Driving conditions. If you're not accustomed to driving on the left, be careful for the first few days, especially when turning corners and at roundabouts (traffic circles). Driving on country lanes can be a pleasurable experience, but be alert for the unexpected: you could find cattle camped in the road, tractors inching along and ambling pedestrians. On zebra crossings (marked by amber beacons), pedestrians have the right of way. Beware of bicycles weaving in and out of town traffic; cyclists make their own rules here.

Speed limits. Unless otherwise marked, the speed limit in the Irish Republic is 60mph (96kmph) on the open road, and it is set at 30 or 40mph (48 or 64kmph) in towns and built-up areas. On motorways the limit is 70mph (113kmph). In Northern Ireland the limit in towns is 30mph (48kmph), 60mph (96kmph) in the country and 70mph (113kmph) on motorways.

Parking. This is becoming more difficult, especially in Dublin and other big cities. Parking meters in Dublin generally have instructions printed on them. Some towns have zones requiring 'discs' or other variations on this time-limit system. Check the signs for regulations.

If you leave your car on a yellow line during business hours you may be fined for parking in a no-parking zone. If you leave your car on a double line, meaning 'no waiting', it may be towed away; and you will have to pay a fine plus towing charges. Be careful of the regulations in Northern Ireland, where some areas are off-limits to cars. You should know that in Northern Ireland the 'no unattended vehicles' warnings really mean business. The security forces don't tow away suspicious cars, they detonate them.

Fuel. In some areas finding a filling station open on a Sunday may be a problem, so it's best to top up on Saturday for weekend excursions. Petrol (gas) is sold by the litre.

Fluid measures

Seat belts. Drivers and front-seat passengers must wear seat belts in the Republic; failure to use them may be punished by a fine. If rear seat belts are fitted, it is compulsory to use them.

Drinking and driving. Police on both sides of the border are strict about this. Any driver suspected of being affected by drink will be subjected to a roadside breathaliser test. Those who fail – and it only takes a pint or two of beer – risk heavy fines, or jail, or both. The crack-down affects visitors as well as residents.

Road signs. Many international picture-signs are used on highways. The road direction signs in the Republic are mostly in English and Gaelic, but in Irish-speaking enclaves the English may be omitted. Traditional road signs give distances in miles but the white-on-green signs are in kilometres (with a small 'km' to remind you).

Some signs may not be comprehensible to visitors:

Ireland	*USA*
Clearway	No parking along highway
Cul de sac	Dead end
Dual carriageway	Divided highway
Layby	Rest area
Level crossing	Rail crossing
Loose chippings	Loose gravel
No overtaking	No passing
Road up	Under construction

| **Roadworks** | Men working |
| **Soft edges** (or **margin**) | Soft shoulder |

Distance

E

ELECTRIC CURRENT

In Ireland the standard current everywhere is 220-volt, a 50-cycle, but you will find that hotels usually have special sockets for shavers, running at both 220 and 110 volts.

Note that it is possible for certain appliances to need a converter, and also that adaptor plugs may be required to fit into Ireland's two types of wall outlets. These can be either three-pin flat or two-pin round.

EMBASSIES and CONSULATES

The Dublin telephone directory lists foreign embassies and consular services under the heading 'Diplomatic and Consular Missions'. Consular agencies in provincial towns are all listed in Part 2 of the directory under the same heading.

The details of the principal embassies and consulates in **Dublin** are as follows:

Australia: Fitzwilton House, Wilton Terrace, Dublin 2; tel. (01) 676 1517.

Canada: 65/68 St Stephen's Green, Dublin 2; tel. (01) 478 1988.

Great Britain: 33 Merrion Road, Dublin 4; tel. (01) 269 5211.

USA: 42 Elgin Road, Dublin 4; tel. (01) 668 8777.

In Northern Ireland:

USA: Queen's House, Queen Street, Belfast 1; tel. (0232) 328239. **125**

EMERGENCIES (See also EMBASSIES and CONSULATES on p.125, MEDICAL CARE on p.130 and POLICE on p.133)

To contact the police, fire brigade or an ambulance in an emergency, dial **999** from any telephone in Ireland (no coin required), and tell the emergency operator which service you need. Have details of your location ready before you make your call.

G

GAY and LESBIAN TRAVELLERS

Nowadays the attitude of younger people in Ireland generally tends to be tolerant towards gay and lesbian people, but some travellers may find there is a slightly more socially conservative attitude in the southern parts of Ireland and some of the more provincial or remote areas of the country.

Various organisations provide advisory services for gay people. They include the Gay Federation, Dublin; tel. (01) 671 0939, and the Reach group for gay Christians on tel. (01) 872 1055. Also, NIGRA (Northern Ireland Gay Rights Association) holds weekly meetings. For information write to NIGRA, c/o PO Box 44, Belfast BT1 ISH; or call the organisation on tel. 0232-664111/325851.

There are also a number of counselling organisations:

Gay Switchboard, Dublin; tel. (01) 872-1055. Open 8-10pm Sunday to Friday, and 3.30-6.30pm Saturday.

Lesbian Line, Dublin; tel. (01) 661-3777. Open 7-9pm Thursday.

GUIDES and TOURS

Guided tours are conducted at some major attractions as part of the admission fee, and a variety of excursions are led by guides, covering major monuments and beauty spots by coach. Tourist offices have schedules; the Dublin office has a list of qualified guides.

LANGUAGE

English is spoken with lilting Irish accents everywhere in Ireland. In the Gaeltacht areas of the west and south, the principal language is Irish, though most people speak fluent English too. Bilingualism is officially encouraged in the Republic. Summer courses in the Irish language are given in the Gaeltacht.

Write to Comhdhail Naisiunta na Gaeilge, 86 Sraid Gardner Iocht, Baile Atha Cliath 1, Republic of Ireland.

Here is a short Irish glossary to help you read the signs:

Irish/Gaelic	*English*
ar(d)	high place
ath	ford of river
baile, bally	hamlet, group of houses, town
beann, ben	mountain peak
cairn	mound of stones on top of a prehistoric tomb
carrick, carrig	rock
cather	fort
clachan, clochan	small group of dwellings; stepping stones across a river; beehive-shaped hut
clon, cluain	meadow
corrach	marsh or low plain
corrie	circular hollow with steep sides
currach	small boat
derry, dare	oak tree or wood
donagh	church
drum, drom	ridge, hillock
dun, doon	fort

127

ennis, inch, innis(h)	island	
keel, kill, caol	narrow	
kil, kill, cill	church; monk's cell	
lough	lake, sea inlet	
mol, mull	height	
ros	promontory or wood	
sceillig, skellig	crag, rock	
sliabh, slieve	mountain	
tulach, tully	hillock	

And here are a few phrases to help you in general, with a rough guide to pronunciation:

Dia dhuit	hello	*diah guich*
slán	goodbye	*slawn*
(many people in Ireland also say 'good luck' meaning 'goodbye')		
oíche mhaith	good night	*e-ha wah*
go raibh maith agat	thank you	*goh rev moh a-gut*
le do thoil	please	*leh doh hol*
tá fáilte romhat	you're welcome	*taw faltcha rowet*
sláinte!	cheers!	*sloyn-tcha*
gam pardún	excuse me	*gum par-doon*
Cá bhuil an ... ?	Where is the ... ?	*koh will on*

LAUNDRY and DRY CLEANING

Hotels in Ireland provide laundry and cleaning services. They often charge extra for 'express' service. There are launderettes, dry cleaning establishments and self-service launderettes in most towns, and you can usually arrange a 'service wash' for a small extra charge.

LOST PROPERTY

The first place to go in search of lost property is the local police station. However, public transport organizations sometimes have their own lost property departments. For items you may have left by accident on trains or buses in Dublin, try the Dublin Bus Lost Property, 98 Marlborough Street, Dublin 1; tel. (01) 720000, or you can contact the Irish Rail Lost Property, Connolly Station, Amiens Street, Dublin 1; tel. (01) 363333.

The main lost property office in Belfast is at Musgrave Street c/o the RUC (Royal Ulster Constabulary) Police Station; tel. (0232) 650222, ext. 26050.

M

MEDIA

Radio and Television. Radio Telefís Eireann (RTE) is state-run and the largest broadcaster in the Republic, though cable television has expanded the choice. Most programmes are in English except for a few Irish or bilingual ones. Foreign films are sometimes shown in the original language with English subtitles. RTE operates three radio stations primarily in English, as well as Raidio na Gaeltachta with an all-Irish programme. The BBC runs five radio stations in Northern Ireland, and there are also commercial channels aimed at audiences north and south of the border.

Transistors and car radios can pick up the principal radio stations of Europe; reception is best at night.

Newspapers. Three national morning papers are published in Dublin – the *Irish Independent*, the *Irish Press* and the *Irish Times*. The *Cork Examiner* is considered a national daily.

Northern Ireland has two morning dailies, the *News Letter* and the *Irish News*. Entertainment news is covered in the *Evening Herald* and *Evening Press* of Dublin, the *Evening Echo* of Cork and the *Belfast Telegraph*. Sunday papers are also useful, and visitors will also find a what's on section in the fortnightly magazine *In Dublin*.

Britain's national daily and Sunday newspapers are sold almost everywhere in the country on the morning of publication. Leading newsagents in the major towns also sell European newspapers and magazines as well as American magazines.

MEDICAL CARE (See also EMERGENCIES on p.126)

Residents of EU countries (formerly EC) are covered by reciprocal health care in Ireland, and visitors from mainland Europe should ensure that they bring a completed E111 form; no form is required for UK visitors. Other nationalities should have some form of hospital insurance – many package tours provide temporary policies.

Hotels usually know which local doctors are available, but in an emergency you can dial **999** to find a doctor on call. In Dublin at least one hospital is always open for emergency cases; again, the operator on 999 can tell you which hospital is on duty.

The Dental Hospital, Lincoln Place, Dublin 2; tel. (01) 6794311, takes dental emergency cases from 9-11am and 2-4pm.

Chemists (pharmacies) operate during shopping hours. A few stay open until 10pm, and some from 11am-1pm or 10pm on Sundays. Details of rota arrangements are given in chemists' windows.

MONEY MATTERS

Currency. The symbol for the Irish pound (or *punt*) of the Republic is abbreviated £; in Northern Ireland the British pound sterling (£) is used. Both are divided into 100 pence (p). British and Irish coins are identically sized and shaped and sometimes slip across the border, but the currencies are no longer interchangeable. Banks everywhere on the island are accustomed to exchanging *punts* and pounds.

Irish banknotes are issued in £5, £10, £20, £50 and also £100 denominations. Coins come in 1p, 2p, 5p, 10p, 20p, 50p and £1.

Exchange facilities. All major banks provide exchange facilities. Major post offices, including the GPO in Dublin, have a bureau de change. Some international travel agencies also change money and traveller's cheques. Be sure to take along your passport as proof of identity when cashing traveller's cheques (see also OPENING HOURS on p.132 for further information).

The O'Connell Street Tourist Information Office in Dublin and the Cork Office in Grand Parade operate money exchange services. **130** The Dublin office will change your money from 9am-5.15pm Monday to Friday, while the Cork office provides this facility from 9am-1.15pm and 2.30-5.15pm Monday to Friday.

Credit cards and traveller's cheques are widely accepted in Irish shops, hotels, restaurants and car-hire firms. **Eurocheques** are also accepted in many hotels and stores and in all banks.

PLANNING YOUR BUDGET

To give you an idea of what to expect, here's a list of average prices in Irish pounds. They can only be approximate, however, as inflation increases relentlessly.

Accommodations: luxury hotel (double room, bath and breakfast) £70-120. Medium hotel (double room, bath and breakfast) £35-55. Guesthouses (double room with bath) £20-40. In town and country homes and farmhouses, bed and breakfast costs £9-15.

Airport transfer: coach to Dublin £2.50, taxi to central Dublin £10.

Babysitter: £5 per hour.

Bicycle rental: £30-40 per week, plus deposit.

Buses: local fares £2.50 (to the most distant suburb). An 8-day rail/bus rambler ticket for unlimited cross-country travel costs £78, a 15-day ticket is £115.

Camping: £7-10 per night.

Car rental (international company): Fiat Uno £45 per day with unlimited mileage, 30p per mile, or £240 per week with unlimited mileage. Opel Kadett £50 per day with unlimited mileage, 34p per mile,or £260 per week with unlimited mileage. Add 12.5 percent tax.

Cigarettes: £2.50 per packet of 20.

Entertainment: cinema tickets cost £2-3.50. Discotheque, cabaret, nightclub entrance fees are £5, theatre tickets are £5-10.

Ferry: Galway-Aran Islands £15 return.

Hairdressers: woman's wash and blow-dry £8, cut £12. Man's cut, wash and blow-dry £12.

Meals and drinks: set-price lunch £6, dinner £10-£30, add a carafe of wine at £9, soft drink £1.20, pint of beer £1.80, whiskey £1.30. **131**

Museums, stately homes: £2.50 admission.

Taxis: minimum charge, Dublin £4, O'Connell Street to Heuston Station £5, Merrion Square to St Patrick's Cathedral £5. You may find a supplement is payable for extra passengers, baggage, etc.

Tours: Dublin city sightseeing, half-day £7. Cork coach tour to the Ring of Kerry £10.

Trains: Dublin-Cork £32.50, weekend return £28. An 8-day rail rambler ticket for unlimited travel is £60, a 15-day ticket is £90.

OPENING HOURS

The opening hours of shops and offices can vary from season to season and according to where they are located.

Shops in the cities are normally open from 9am-5.30pm Monday to Saturday; country towns have one early closing day. However, the big shopping centres often stay open until 9pm on Thursday and Friday. Smaller shops, particularly groceries and newsagents, often open on Sundays and many stay open until 1pm. Also, some Dublin suburbs have 24-hour shops, which are open all day and all night.

Offices and businesses operate from 9am-5.30pm Monday to Friday (and on Saturdays as well in some cases). Tourist information offices are open from 10am-6pm with longer summer hours in the busiest places.

Banks. In general banks are open 10am-12.30pm and 1.30-3pm Monday to Friday. Most towns have a late opening day once a week (Thursday in Dublin), when banks stay open until 5pm. You'll also find that many banks remain open over the lunch hour. In Northern Ireland banks are open from 10am-3.30pm. Outside Belfast, branches may close for lunch. The bank at Dublin Airport is open every day of the year except Christmas, from 6.45am-9pm in the winter and **132** until 10pm in the summer.

Pubs. Licensing hours have been streamlined. In the Republic, the winter hours are 10.30am-11pm, with an extra half hour in summer. On Sundays all year, pubs are open from 12.30-2pm and from 4-11pm. In addition, there is half-an-hour drinking-up time in the evenings all year round. In Northern Ireland, pubs are open Monday to Saturday 11.30am-11pm, all year.

Sunday opening is a relatively new departure, and is followed by some pubs, which now open from 12.30-2.30pm, and from 7-10pm, all year. In addition, there is half-an-hour drinking-up time.

Museums, stately homes, etc. Museums and stately homes follow no general rule except that visiting hours will often be curtailed in winter. There are no universal days when these institutions are closed, though Sunday, Monday or Tuesday are the most probable. To avoid disappointment always check first with the nearest tourist information office.

P

PHOTOGRAPHY

All those green fields, blue skies and white clouds make beautiful pictures, but if you should run out of film, you'll easily find all the well-known brands on sale. Be sure to ask permission before you take photos in museums and historic churches; sometimes flashbulbs are forbidden. Military bases are off-limits to photographers. Please note that in Northern Ireland you should avoid pointing your camera, or anything else, at personnel or installations of the security forces.

POLICE (See also EMERGENCIES on p.126)

The civic guard (police force) of the Irish Republic is the *Garda Siochana*, known as the *Garda* (pronounced 'gorda'). In Northern Ireland the police force is the Royal Ulster Constabulary, or the RUC as it is commonly known. In case of emergency, telephone **999**, in both the Republic and Northern Ireland.

133

PUBLIC HOLIDAYS

Shops, banks, official departments and restaurants are closed on public holidays. If a date falls on a Sunday, then the following Monday is taken in lieu.

In the Republic of Ireland and Northern Ireland:

1 January	*New Year's Day*
17 March	*St. Patrick's Day*
last w/e in May (movable date)	*Good Friday/Easter Monday*
25 December	*Christmas Day*
26 December	*Boxing Day*

In the Republic of Ireland only:

first Monday in June	*June Bank Holiday*
last Monday in August	*August Bank Holiday*
last Monday in October	*October Bank Holiday*

In Northern Ireland only:

first Monday in May	*May Day*
last Monday in May	*Spring Bank Holiday*
12 July	*Orangemen's Day*
last Monday in August	*Summer Bank Holiday*

R

RELIGION

About 95 percent of the people in the Irish Republic are Catholic. Many go to Sunday Mass, which can be heard in Dublin almost any time, from 6am-9pm, in English, and sometimes in Irish.

Dublin's cathedrals are of the (Anglican) Church of Ireland, and schedules of the services at these and other Protestant churches can be found in hotels, and in Saturday papers (see p.129). Dublin has Protestant, Greek Orthodox, Jewish and Islamic places of worship.

In Northern Ireland, Catholics make up less than a third of the population, but they outnumber the largest single Protestant group, the Presbyterians, as well as the Church of Ireland.

The ecclesiastic capital of Ireland is Armagh, situated in the North with two cathedrals, one Catholic and the other Church of Ireland. Both are called St Patrick's.

TIME DIFFERENCES

Ireland sets its clocks one hour ahead of GMT (Greenwich Mean Time) from mid-March to the end of October, but the rest of the year the clocks are set to GMT.

TIPPING

Most hotels and restaurants include a service charge, so tipping is unnecessary. However, good or extra service from bellboys, filling-station attendants etc deserves an appropriate extra gratuity.

TOILETS/RESTROOMS

Public conveniences abound in Irish towns, and are well signposted. The only hitch is that the gender signs on doors in the Republic may be printed in Gaelic, not English. *Mna* should not be misconstrued as a misprint for 'men'; it's Gaelic for 'ladies'. *Fir* means 'gentlemen'.

TOURIST INFORMATION OFFICES

Tourist information offices all over Ireland provide full travel information and advice, booklets, maps and a comprehensive hotel reservation service (for a small charge), which can extend to booking novel horse-drawn caravans and self-drive cabin cruisers. The offices are usually open from 10am-6pm, although many local ones operate only in the summer. For enquiries, write to one of the following:

Irish Tourist Board, Bord Failte, PO Box 273, Dublin 8.

Northern Ireland Tourist Board, St Anne's Court, North Street, Belfast BT1 IND.

You may also address your enquiries to offices of the **British Tourist Authority** the world over.

TRANSPORT (See also MONEY MATTERS on p.130)

Buses. The state-run *Bus Eireann* operates an extensive network of local, provincial and express bus routes, including full cross-border services in conjunction with Northern Ireland's Ulsterbus Ltd. The service to the various destinations of tourist interest is increased in the summer. You can buy a handy, pocket-sized timetable at bus stations and tourist information offices. *Bus Atha Cliath/Dublin Bus* runs Dublin Area Services. A separate book lists all bus and train routes in the Dublin district.

The bus services in Ireland cover almost every town and village. 'Expressway' buses provide a non-stop inter-city service, while the so-called 'Provincial' vehicles make frequent stops in rural areas.

Iarnród Eireann-Irish Rail and *Bus Eireann* sell a rambler ticket, valid for either 8 or 15 days of unlimited cross-country bus and rail travel. There is also an overlander ticket with 15 days of unlimited travel in the Republic and also with Ulsterbus and Northern Ireland Railways (see also TRAINS below).

On some buses in the Republic the destination is indicated in Irish only, so if you don't want to arrive in Gaillimh (Galway) instead of Gleann Garbh (Glengarriff), you'd better learn the correct Gaelic name before you start out. You will find that the timetable book has a useful glossary.

The busiest bus routes in the cities use double-deckers, on which you take a seat and wait for the conductor to come and collect the proper fare. On single-deckers you must pay the driver as you enter. Queues (lines) are taken seriously, and you should note that in Ireland the official Queueing Regulations of 1961 rule that six or more persons waiting for a bus must form a queue two abreast in an orderly manner. The queue faces the direction from which the bus will arrive, except where the bus stop sign indicates otherwise.

Trains. Passenger train lines in Ireland have been cut back to the main routes, but cross-country services to and from Dublin are both quick and comfortable. The main inter-city routes have air-conditioned, sound-proofed expresses.

There are two classes on through-trains: Standard (2nd class) and Super Standard (1st class). *Iarnród Eireann-Irish Rail*, which is the Irish railway company, sells eight-day and 15-day rambler tickets, good for unlimited rail travel, or rail and bus travel at higher prices. A practical book of train timetables is on sale at railway stations and tourist offices.

Note: Dublin has two main-line railway stations (Heuston Station and Connolly Station), as well as a commuter-line station, so be sure to check in advance for the correct terminal.

Some trip times on express trains:

Dublin-Belfast:	2 hr 10 min
Dublin-Cork:	2 hr 30 min
Dublin-Galway:	2 hr 50 min
Dublin-Waterford:	2 hr 35 min

Ireland has now joined the group of countries which are honouring the **Eurailpass**, a flat-rate unlimited mileage ticket, valid for any first-class rail travel in Western Europe outside the UK. The **Eurail Youthpass** is similar to the Eurailpass, but offers second-class travel at a cheaper rate to anyone who is under 26. This ticket is available to visitors from outside Europe.

Taxis. Irish taxis may be found cruising the streets, but most park at designated ranks waiting for clients. Taxis can also be contacted by telephone (see the classified telephone directory under *Taxicabs – Ranks and Shelters*).

Many towns have radio-dispatched taxis, but these usually charge extra for the mileage to pick up the client. Fares can vary from town to town. Dublin and Cork have metered taxis while smaller towns have standard fares or charges by agreement.

Very few Dublin taxi drivers have been known to add imaginary supplements to the fare. Note that you should pay only the charge on the meter plus, if applicable, supplements for extra passengers, additional luggage, waiting time, and trips on public holidays or after midnight.

Radio-cab dispatchers in Dublin can be reached on any of the following numbers; tel: 676 1111, 668 3333, 676 6666, 478 3333 and 677 2222.

Boats and Ferries. With over 3,000 miles (4,800km) of coastline and 9,000 miles (14,480km) of rivers and streams, Ireland is a boater's paradise. You might hire a fishing boat to take advantage of the excellent fresh-water and sea fishing, or enjoy the country's scenic splendours in a rented cruiser (normally available with two to eight berths).

No boating permit is needed for travelling on the Shannon, and all companies offer a free piloting lesson. The points of departure include Carrick-on-Shannon, Athlone, Banagher and Killaloe.

The rugged islands off the coast of Ireland are rich in folklore, antiquities and eye-catching natural wonders (especially birdlife). The Irish Tourist Board issues an information sheet – *Island Boat Services* – listing numerous possibilities, including scheduled ferries. The Aran Islands are only a 30-mile steamer ride from Galway; and crossings can also be made from Rossaveal, May to September, and from Doolin in County Clare.

There are connections by air, as well, which are around 20 minutes. Garinish Island, which is noted for its exuberant vegetation, is only 10 minutes away from Glengarriff (County Cork). Bad weather may interrupt ferry services.

TRAVELLERS WITH DISABILITIES

A lot of progress has been made in recent years to provide more facilities for disabled travellers. Ramps have been provided, giving access to many community buildings, and much of the public transport system has been geared up to welcoming disabled people.

The more modern city buses in Dublin have facilities for wheelchair users to board the bus, and trains have level entry access. Airlines are also friendly towards disabled passengers.

Public awareness of disabled people has increased enormously over the years too, so that there is now a much greater willingness to help disabled people.

For advice and information, contact the **National Council for the Blind in Dublin**, tel (01) 830 7033, and the **National Chaplaincy for the Deaf**, also in Dublin, tel (01) 830 5744.

TRAVELLING TO IRELAND

It is advisable to consult a travel agent for the latest information on tariffs and other arrangements as well as writing to the local tourist offices for information in advance (see p.135).

From Great Britain
BY AIR

Visitors and tourists can fly in from airports across the UK to Dublin, Shannon, Cork, Waterford and Knock in Ireland. New routes are opening all the time, so it may be worth checking with the airline of your choice for information on the most convenient connections to Ireland.

Charter Flights and Package Tours. A wide array of packages is currently available for travellers and visitors, making good use of the varied holiday accommodation Ireland has to offer: whether it be cottages and farmhouses, driving your own romantic horse-drawn caravan, cruising down the river, or even other, more traditional forms of self-catering accommodation, there will be something in Ireland for everyone.

Some airlines offer fly-drive tours, as well as special fares which may include your flight and all the transport to and from your final destination in Ireland. Check with the airline of your choice.

BY SEA

There are various routes you can take to reach Ireland by sea, depending on the area you wish to drive through in Britain.

Passenger and car ferries sail frequently from Holyhead to Dublin and Dun Laoghaire. There is also a regular service from Fishguard and Pembroke to Rosslare Harbour, and from Swansea to Cork. Ferries shuttle several times a day from Cairnryan and Stanraer to Larne (near Belfast).

Those touring Ireland without a car might want to buy a rambler ticket (giving you 8 or 15 days of unlimited bus and rail travel) or **139** an overlander ticket (which will allow you 15 days of bus and rail travel, including Northern Ireland on just the one ticket), which can be bought either at home or in Ireland from *Bus Eireann* or *Iarnród Eireann-Irish Rail*. Inter-Rail Cards are valid 30 days in Europe for young people who are under 26 and for senior citizens over 65.

From North America

BY AIR

Travellers from almost every major American city and several major Canadian cities can make connections to Dublin or Shannon through New York or Boston. Regular services are also available to Knock.

Charter Flights and Package Tours. Charter flights to Shannon, with connections to Dublin, feature even further air-fare reductions. The tourist boards have full details of charter flights.

W

WEIGHTS and MEASURES

(For fluid and distance measures, see DRIVING on p.122)

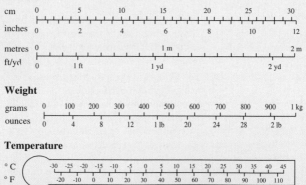

Length

Weight

Temperature

WOMEN TRAVELLERS

Women travelling alone in Ireland need to be as cautious in some areas of Ireland's major cities as they are in comparable areas in the major cities in their own home countries.

To ensure your safety, take a friend with you if possible, or decide to travel through dark and lonely areas by taxi. Inform yourself in advance about the times of the last trains, buses etc, and have enough funds with you to pay for the full cost of your return travel by taxi, if necessary. Also, take some relevant telephone numbers with you for taxis, the police, and some advisory organisations.

In Dublin, the area north of the River Liffey and west of the city centre is best avoided at night if you are alone. Similarly, the centres of Cork and Limerick are best avoided at night by women travelling on their own.

For further information and helpful advice contact the **Women's Information Network** in Dublin, tel (01) 679 4700. Alternatively, you could write to either of the following for advice prior to starting your journey:

Women's Aid, PO Box 791, Dublin 6; tel. (01) 496 1002.

YMCA, 64 Lower Baggot Street, Dublin 2 (hostel), and 49 St John's Road, Dublin 4; tel. 269 2205.

Y

YOUTH HOSTELS

The Irish Youth Hostels Association runs 50 hostels in the Republic of Ireland. Membership cards are required, and these are issued by national youth hostel associations overseas.

An official handbook is available from the **Youth Hostels Association** (Head Office), 61 Mountjoy Street, Dublin 1.

There are a dozen youth hostels in Northern Ireland. Details can be requested from **Youth Hostel Information**, 56 Bradbury Place, Belfast BT7 1RU.

Index

Where there is more than one entry, numbers in **bold** refer to the main entry listed.

019/408 REV